Self-Publishing for Profit

HOW TO GET YOUR BOOK OUT OF YOUR
HEAD AND INTO THE STORES

Chris Kennedy

Chris Kennedy Publishing
Virginia Beach, VA

Chris Kennedy/Chris Kennedy Publishing
2052 Bierce Dr.
Virginia Beach, VA 23454
www.chriskennedypublishing.com

Ordering Information:
Quantity sales. Special discounts are available on quantity purchases by corporations, associations, and others. For details, contact the "Special Sales Department" at the address above.

Self-Publishing for Profit/Chris Kennedy. —1st ed.
ISBN 978-1-942936-00-8

Contents

i

I would like to thank Linda, Jennie, Beth and Dan, who took the time to critically read this work and make it better. I would also like to thank my mother; without her steadfast belief in me, I would not be where I am today. Thank you. This book is dedicated to my wife and children, who sacrificed their time with me so that I could write it.

Author Notes

All prices and statistics referenced in this book were current as of January 10, 2015. Please consult the websites indicated for up-to-date pricing information.

Earnings Disclaimer: There is no promise or representation that you will make a certain amount of sales, or any sales, as a result of the techniques that are outlined within this book. Any earnings, revenue or results using these strategies are estimates and there is no guarantee you will have the same results. You accept the risks that earnings differ by individual and situation. The use of the information, products and services referenced in this book should be based on your own due diligence, and you agree that the author is not liable for your success or failure. If you disagree, please return this book for a refund.

Self-Publishing as a Career

Welcome to the world of self-publishing. I'm excited that you've put your trust in me; I'm going to help get your book out of your head and into the stores, where you can make some great money. Not long ago, I was in your shoes, unpublished and doubting myself, but now I have seven books in print. Until recently, that's something no one would ever have thought I would (or even that I *could*) do. I didn't have a Creative Writing degree, and I didn't know anyone in the publishing industry. Heck, I didn't know anything about self-publishing either. If I can do it, starting out with nothing but a story, you can, too. Let's get started!

Chapter 1 – Why Self-Publishing?

How did I get into self-publishing? Let me take you back two years. I was broke and unemployed. I finally found a job, but things didn't get any better. My hourly wage wasn't enough to cover all of my family's monthly expenses, much less the debt we had run up in my nine months of unemployment. We had already gone through one of the retirement accounts I had set up in my 20 years of Navy service, and we had just started on the other.

I also had a son who was a senior in high school and two daughters who were sophomores; in three years I would have three college tuitions to pay. As I went through the financial aid process with my son, I found out that I was in that no man's land where I now made enough money in my new job that I no longer qualified for tuition assistance; however, I didn't make enough that I could actually pay his tuition. I had too many obligations and not enough income. I needed something else, or my family was going to go under.

Does this sound familiar?

It was at this point that I found self-publishing, which is something that anyone can do. That doesn't mean it's "easy," but then again, what worth doing ever is? The difference between self-publishing and every other industry I have ever worked in is that there is no one to tell you "no." The only person that can stop you is you.

Of course, it's not as simple as just throwing a few lines of prose onto a page and then sitting back to watch the dollars flow into your bank account; however, self-publishing is a process that anyone can do and make money with, *if you have a plan.*

Let me say that again because it bears repeating. Making money in self-publishing is a process that *anyone can do if they have a plan.* You don't need contacts in the industry. You don't need a rich uncle to bankroll you by purchasing the first 100,000 copies of your novel to get you onto the New York Times Bestsellers' List. You don't even need a Creative Writing or English degree.

Sure, it's helpful if you have those things, but do you need them? No, you don't need *any* of them. I didn't have a single one when I started my self-publishing career, and within seven months I was generating monthly royalties equal to a six-figure yearly income. How was I able to do that? I had a plan. I knew what I was going to do, how I was going to do it and when each of the events in my plan was going to happen. Before I sold my first book, I already had a plan for the first year and most of the second. I was successful because of this plan, and you can be successful, too, because I'm going to share my plan with you.

"But wait," you ask; "if you share your plan, won't that dilute your ability to make money, and decrease how much I can make, too?" No, it won't. The secret to my success is that we live in a digital economy, and more and more people every day are looking for digital stories. Why spend $25 on a hard cover book, or even $12 on a paperback, that you're just going to read once and then dispose of? Wouldn't it be better, *and cheaper,* to read a digital story that is only $2.99 or $3.99? The traditional publishing industry continues to sell their ebooks for the same price as their paper copies, giving you a tremendous competitive marketing advantage;

your book can undercut their prices, making it attractive to readers world-wide, regardless of the fact that no one has ever heard of you.

"But wait," you say. "How am I going to sell books in foreign countries? I don't have an agent!" I'll share my agent with you, the same agent that has helped me sell books in 12 countries outside of the United States. It's easy to sell your books world-wide, and I'll show you how.

Self-Publishing for Profit is a guide for those that are interested in self-publishing, whether you want a career in publishing or just a way to make a few extra dollars on the side. This book shouldn't be seen as the only way to do it because there is no such thing as "one size fits all." If people tell you that you "must" do something a certain way, beware! They probably don't have your best interests at heart.

This book will give you all of the essentials you need to get started, and it will serve as a guide as you grow and prosper in the trade. Self-publishing is the one career I know of where you get to decide every facet of how you carry out your business. There is no one to make you do things a certain way, no one to set your hours (for good or bad) and no one to determine your success *besides you*. You alone determine your success or failure. That is a powerful statement. Almost everyone would love to have a job where that is true.

Unfortunately, not everyone will thrive in this environment. Some people need to have rules and structure, and they need to be led from place to place. "Be at work at 8:00." "Sit here and do this..." Some people don't have the discipline to be their own business owner. The best thing is, that's OK. If you are one of these people, this book will still be useful to you, and you will be able to use it to make money in self-publishing. Maybe quite a bit of money if you follow the principles I'll show you.

Other people are going to thrive in this environment. If you are one of these people, you have the potential to be *very* successful if you do the things I am going to teach you. I started with nothing. I didn't know anyone in the publishing industry, and I had never written a story outside of an assignment in a high school English class. I am, however, good at research, and I put together a plan for marketing my books and continuing to write new books that I knew was repeatable. Ten months after publishing my first book, I sold over 7,700 copies. At an average royalty of $2.65 a book, that is over *$20,000 in a single month*. In no other job could I have done that.

I once had someone tell me, "You'll never get rich working for someone else." That is the truth...but how many occupations allow you to work for yourself and give you a real chance at success?

I know of only one. Self-publishing.

I've organized this book into a number of units that deal with the most important topics for starting a career in self-publishing. The information is presented in such a manner that it not only makes sense, but gives you the tools to act on this new-found knowledge, too. Don't worry! I'm not going to just dump a bunch of information on you without explaining and helping you to understand the key points needed to be successful. I did this, and you can too!

The hardest part about this process is that you have to be doing a number of things at once. Generally, the units are arranged in the order that you should approach them, although some sections will overlap, and there will be some repetition. If something is mentioned in a number of sections, it is probably something that's important to your success, and you should pay close attention.

You can spend nothing and have a book that doesn't sell; you can just as easily spend a ton of cash and achieve the same lack of results. The key is to know what to spend money on and what to do yourself. At the end of the process you need a well-edited book with a professional-looking cover and a great description. By developing a great product, you are creating something that sells and will make your marketing job easier. As such, the units on editing and book cover design **SHOULD NOT BE SKIPPED**. You owe it to yourself to read these topics. If you think you already know it and just skip down to the marketing sections, you are doing yourself a tremendous disservice. Readers on the internet are savvy, and it won't take many horrible reviews to relegate your book to the dustbin of history. With tons of free books in the marketplace, you need a quality book to get paid what you want.

If I could give you only one piece of advice from everything I've learned, it's that self-publishing is a marathon, not a sprint. Success will not be achieved in a day or a month. There are going to be good days, where it looks like you have finally broken through, followed by days where it looks like everyone hates you. People will say mean things to you and about you, and they will make you wonder why you are wasting your time publishing. **DON'T GIVE UP!** I've found out that, a lot of times, they haven't even read your book! How about that? It happens, so don't spend too much time or anxiety on it. Okay...you're probably going to get upset about the first bad review you get (I did), but whine about it for a few minutes _and then move on_. Get back to work. No matter what you do, there are going to be people that say bad things about you. Remember, it's a marathon. Ignore them and get back to work. You can do this.

I've found that the biggest obstacle to your success is you, if you start believing the things you are going to hear along the way. Why is that? Because if you start believing everything you hear, it's going to poison your mind (remember, it's a marathon); that's why I want to talk about some of these things first and get them out of the way.

Chapter 2 – The 4 Great Lies of Self-Publishing

The first thing that you have to come to grips with in your new career is the nay-sayers that you will run into on the road to success. Some of them you may know, while others will never be more than a screen name like "tkigh" or "Sneffens"…or the dreaded "Amazon Customer." Some may even be in your own head. Whether you know who they are or not, all are cancerous; they only exist to plant the seeds of doubt in your mind and keep you from being successful. Before we can talk about writing and publishing, it's important to talk about being in the right frame of mind because that is one of the main reasons new authors fail.

I struggled with things I heard on a number of occasions as I went through the process, especially as I got closer and closer to publishing my first book. Oftentimes, I was my own biggest critic, and I threw up plenty of my own roadblocks. Without the support of my wife, I would probably have succumbed to them, and I doubt that *Red Tide* would ever have been published.

What are these seeds of doubt? They are the untruths you will hear in the publishing industry. We all hear them; we all worry about them. You need to be aware of them so you can get past them. Watch out for people telling you the following:

1. You're doing it wrong. There's only one 'right' way to do it.
2. You can't do that. If you do, it will kill your career.
3. It's too late to get into the business. You've already missed out.
4. Self-publishing is too hard. You don't have what it takes.

There are other obstacles that we'll talk about in later sections of this book (I already mentioned reviews; who knew there were so many haters in the world?), but these are the first big barriers that have to be dealt with. An author's mind is fertile ground for new ideas; it will grow doubts just as easily as it does plots for future novels.

You're probably saying, "Why do I want to know about this? Just show me how to publish!" I'm starting with this because you *will* hear these things, and you need to be able to deal with them. I know many authors who quit writing because they chose to believe what they heard. It almost happened to me, so I'm addressing these things now, at the start, *so it won't happen to you!*

The First Lie—There Is Only One Way

One of the first things you're going to hear as a beginning author is that there is only one way to do it. It doesn't matter whether the topic's writing, publishing or marketing, there's just one way to do it...regardless of what "it" is. When people say this, what they really mean is if you do it any way other than *their* way, you're not going to be successful. A lot of times they are authors who were traditionally published; to them, there only is one way...the old way that they knew, not the new ways that currently exist.

Why do people say things like this? Because it used to be true. Before the advent of self-publishing, there really was only one way to get published. You wrote and submitted your work to agents until you improved your craft enough to land one, at which point your agent would try to sell your books to publishers. And then, at some time in the distant future, you got published. Agents and publishers had all of the power, and authors had none. By keeping things this way, they were able to force authors to accept contracts that were not in our best interest. We could either play by their rules, or we could find a different vocation.

Times have changed with the advent of self-publishing, and authors can now publish in a number of ways. In fact, there are at least five main paths you can travel, with so many ways of combining various aspects of these paths that the actual number of possibilities is endless. Here are the five.

The first option is traditional publishing. Just because you *can* self-publish doesn't mean that everyone *should.* Some authors may be more content with the traditional method and the support it provides. An editor helps with your prose, and there's a design process to build your cover. It's all very comfortable.

It's also very *long*; even if you get onto an editor's "Fast Track," it's still going to take you years to get published. Yes, years. With an "s" at the end. It's probably going to be at least two years, and all of the other problems still apply. You have to find an agent who loves your book. Then the agent has to find a publisher who also loves it. There will be changes made to your book, which may or may not cause you angst. You will have to accept a contract where you only get a tiny fraction of the revenue that your book earns, and you're going to be expected to do the majority of your marketing yourself. Traditional publishing is going through a difficult time, and it's probably going to get worse before it gets better. There will be imprints that merge or shut down, and your book could fall through the cracks of this upheaval.

Still, if you *have* to see your book on the shelf of a bookstore near you (for the brief period that it will be there), then you may want to go down the traditional publishing path. This path still exists, but with all of the drawbacks, traditional publishing wasn't the right choice for me. You can also get your books on store shelves without having them traditionally published; we'll discuss that later.

The second option is small press publishing. This is somewhat like the traditional route, but usually removes the agent from the process. There are pros and cons with this method...as well as a greater chance of getting taken to the cleaners since you no longer have an agent watching out for your rights. The contract you sign will be the key to how well you do. While small publishers are usually more likely to work with you (depending on the contract you sign), the editing and book cover design may not be as good as you would have received at one of the larger publishers. I would be *especially* leery of any publishing house that wants you to give them a lot of money up front to get your book published. There are many disreputable small publishers out there that make their money from authors as well as readers. Caveat emptor—let the buyer beware. Before you sign anything with a small press, ALWAYS do an internet search on the company and find out what other people are saying about it. If you can, another good idea is to talk to some of the authors who use that publisher to find out about their experiences.

The third option is to self-publish and hire out everything. This method, along with the next two, are all aspects of self-publishing; they differ in how much the author does and how much he or she contracts out. At one end of the continuum is the "Hire Everything" choice where the author does nothing but write, and everything else required for publication is contracted out. Is this a viable option? Yes. There are a number of author services companies that will take a manuscript through the entire publication process. One of their consultants will develop a publishing strategy for your book, match your requirements with their specialists and manage the project for you from concept to delivery.

If you have good project management skills, you could also pursue this approach by hiring a group of freelancers instead. There are websites such as Writer.ly and Bibliocrunch that allow you to post a project and then select from a number of freelance professionals who will complete the tasks required. Worried about the legitimacy of a freelancer or a group? The Science Fiction and Fantasy Writers of America, with support from the Mystery Writers of America and the Horror Writers Association, maintains an extensive database of questionable literary agents, publishers, independent editors, writers' services, contests, publicity services, and others called Writer Beware at http://www.sfwa.org/other-resources/for-authors/writer-beware/ that can be used to avoid disreputable services.

If you have a large backlist (books that are already written and awaiting publication) or you're just not interested in participating in the publishing process (and you don't mind paying for someone else to do it), this may be the right method for you. You can continue to create new books while someone else handles the entire publishing process.

If you don't have a lot of start-up money or a sizable backlist, this may not be the right option for you, as it comes with costs, not all of which may be apparent up front. First, you are going to pay for things that you could have easily done yourself. For most authors just starting out, this is a big consideration. Also, when you contract out the publishing process to someone else, there is a loss of control. Instead of having things done when you want, you are now at the mercy of how well someone else meets timelines and deadlines. Will they have the same drive and work ethic that you would have put into the project? Maybe...but, then again, maybe not. They certainly won't be as vested in the success of the book as you are.

Finally, by turning over control of everything, you lose out on the self-development that comes with being involved in the process. I have become a much better author by being involved in the editing process. If I had given my book to someone else for editing, I wouldn't have learned many of the things I now know about fiction writing. Similarly, you learn about marketing and cover design by being involved in the process. How can you own your own brand if someone else is creating it for you? As you can see, you lose out on a lot by giving up control of the process; only you can decide if the costs are worth the time that you gain from contracting everything out.

As with the other paths, authors also need to look out for scams when they follow this path. Just because an author services organization is a big company or is associated with a large publisher doesn't necessarily give it credibility. For example, Charman-Anderson noted in May of 2013 that several authors had filed a class action lawsuit against Penguin and its self-publishing services provider, Author Solutions, seeking damages of more than $5 million for deceptive practices. Other horror stories abound; thoroughly research any company that you do business with prior to signing a contract.

How do you do this research? Go online and look at what people are saying, especially in writer's forums and Writer Beware. If there is a problem, people *will* be talking about it. As with the small presses, you should be suspicious of any company that asks for heaps of money up front. If you are unsure about the company, ask for a trial, as many of the author services companies will give you a limited trial run. That doesn't mean they'll edit your first book for free if you promise to bring them your second book; what it *does* mean is they might edit your first chapter and give you feedback without obligation. If you get a sample of their work first, you will be better prepared to judge the full-length product and compare the services offered by different companies.

Be prepared to pay if you make this choice. Editing alone will cost in the thousands of dollars (at least $1,500 for the copy-editing of an 80,000 word novel). How much it actually costs will depend on your manuscript's length and the type of editing you are looking for (developmental editing to improve plot/character, line editing to improve your prose, copy editing to catch grammatical and spelling mistakes, or just proofreading to look for typos and punctuation). Before deciding to go this route, you need to think about how much money your book is likely to bring in. If you are going to spend $2,000 on editing, and you're only planning on making $2.00 a copy, you'll need to sell 1,000 copies just to break even. Don't spend more than you can afford to lose.

The fourth option is to "Do Everything Yourself," where the author is responsible for, you guessed it, everything. The author writes the book, develops the book cover and blurbs, and trades off with friends or a critique group for proofing/editing. When the book is ready to publish, the author puts it on the bookstore sites and then gets working on the next book while simultaneously promoting the first.

Is it possible to do everything yourself? Absolutely. In fact, this is how many authors start when they have limited funding. If nothing else, it's the cheap way to go. If you aren't worried about having an International Standard Book Number, or ISBN, to track and identify your book (we'll talk about why you should be), there aren't that many areas where you *have* to spend money (except for a business license if it's required where you live). There is a steep learning curve with this method, but all of the revenue that comes in is yours. There are a lot of things to do, but you acquire a very "hands-on" knowledge of writing and the publishing business that will make you stronger in the long run. This is a great place to start, as you learn the ins and outs of all of publishing's aspects. This book will show you how to do everything yourself. If you decide to contract out pieces of your business (such as cover design), you can, but you will be better prepared if you know how to do everything yourself.

The fifth option is to self-publish and contract out as needed. In between the two extremes are the independent publishers who know their strengths and weaknesses. They handle the things they do well, and they contract out when it makes more sense for someone else to do them. These publishers are true businessmen and women; decisions are made based on what makes the most financial sense.

On the positive side, this method will let you maximize your strengths; however, you have to know enough about the individual facets of publishing to know when you're getting a high quality product from a freelancer, and when you're getting crap. For example, if you don't have a degree in graphic design, it's a good idea to contract out the cover. You still have to know what makes a great cover, though, or your book sales are going to suffer. The one drawback to this method versus doing everything yourself is that there are some upfront costs (which is why many authors start on Path 4 and move to Path 5 once they've made some money).

In addition to these options, the publishing industry continues to grow and develop, and there are new ways coming of which authors will need to be aware. In some places, authors are forming co-ops to share their skills. Others are grouping together to form their own publishing companies, so that they can have more clout in the promotion, sales and distribution of their books. By keeping up with trends in the industry, you'll be better prepared to take advantage of opportunities when they come.

The bottom line is that an author should pursue the publishing path that makes the most sense for his or her own situation. Ultimately, there is only one right way for you to do something; it's the way that makes you the most money and makes you the happiest along the way. It isn't going to be someone else's way, nor is it likely to be mine, and that's okay. In time, you are going to find out what works best for you, and THAT is the only right way.

The Second Lie—The Death of Your Career

It's funny to have to talk about the death of your career with someone that may just be starting out, but it's important for you to know that your options for success are wide open. Just as there's no "one way" to do everything, you also need to be aware that there is nothing you can do that will kill your career, so you shouldn't be afraid to experiment. It's not possible to kill your career as an author unless you decide to stop writing. You *can* make mistakes that may cost you money or make you look bad, but you can't kill your career. Why not? Glad you asked; let's look at a couple of examples.

"I did this thing that an editor or agent said not to do. Now they're going to hate me forever." Editors and agents get hundreds of submissions every day. They aren't going to remember that you broke one of their rules unless you did something stupid like threatening them (in which case they *should* remember you, and maybe even get a restraining order). But remember you because you sent in a submission when it said "Agented Submissions Only?" Not likely. Besides, you don't need either editors or agents if you self-publish.

But what if you publish a bad story? That will kill your career, right?

No, a bad story won't kill your career. All that will happen is that your book will sell a few copies, get bad reviews and make you a little money, and then people will stop buying it because of the bad reviews. If that happens, you can pull the book off Amazon and the other ebook retailers and fix whatever is wrong. Maybe the cover is inappropriate. Maybe the book needs better editing. Whatever the problem, you can fix the issues and then resubmit your book (with a different name if you need to). In all likelihood, very few people will remember the first book, or you. With all of the hundreds of thousands of books that are published annually, how could they?

But what if your story was SO bad, so absolutely horrific that it caused every single person on the planet to hate both the book and YOU, the author, personally. Your career would be done then, right? Nope. Ever heard of a pen name? You can write under a new name, and no one will ever know that you and "that other person" are associated (unless you tell them).

There are always critics out there. While they might not hate your book, they will be more than happy to point out errors in it. That won't kill your career either. Odds are, no matter how many times you have people proof your book, it will go out with mistakes. How many mistakes have you found in books from the big publishers? I find between two and five errors in every book I read. Getting it "perfect" is nearly impossible. If you find something wrong with a book once it's published, it's not going to kill your career. Just fix the problem and replace the manuscript on the retailer's website with an updated copy. Most people will never even know.

The Third Lie—You Missed Your Chance!

Okay, so your career is alive, but now someone tells you that you have missed the boat, and self-publishing has left you behind; it's too late because other people have already "won." It's not true. Self-publishing is here to stay, and could very well become the dominant form of publishing as we proceed further into the digital age. The industry may change, but the only way you'll be in a position to take advantage of the new opportunities is if you are writing.

Besides, you don't have to worry about being left behind or having missed out. The industry is doing well, and new authors are starting up all the time. It wasn't too long ago that a new author named Chris Kennedy published his first book. He didn't miss the boat, and neither have you. Also, you don't have to worry about being left behind, as it's not a race. Don't compare yourself to anyone other than yourself, and you'll be fine. Set reasonable goals, build a plan to achieve them and start writing. Don't worry about what success (or lack of success) others are having, aside from studying what is working for them so you can use it to benefit your career.

Self-publishing is the one career where YOU set the goals, and YOU define what is possible. My original plan was to sell 50 copies of my first book, 100 copies of my second book and 500 copies of my third book. I didn't plan for writing to be profitable until my third book. I built a plan to support this. Did it have room for growth if things went well? Yes, but it was based on numbers I thought were realistic for a never-before-published author. Since then, the first book has sold 5,000 copies, the second 4,000 copies and the third 16,000. This huge jump in sales has given me the opportunity to accelerate my plans...a lot.

I don't compare myself to others. I do the things I can do, when I can do them, and I try to set myself up for success. Sometimes I have bad days. Maybe it's because I let a bad review get to me (even though I know better) or I found a major error on a book that had been published for over a year (which happened). When I have a bad day I get up the next day and start again. Even though I just started last year, I wasn't too late. Neither are you.

The Fourth Lie—It's Too Hard

Finally, there's the greatest lie of all: "You'll never be successful with self-publishing because it's just too hard." This lie is insidious because it is always in the back of your mind, giving you an easy way out when things get hard.

Just like "you missed the boat," this lie gives you permission not to try.

Is self-publishing hard? Yes, absolutely, because everything is on you. Conversely, that's also the best part. Since you are responsible for everything, you know where to place the blame if something doesn't get done. You won't be let down by someone else because you are the prime contractor for everything. That makes it difficult since there are a lot of things that have to be done. There is, however, a difference between 'hard' and 'impossible.' Is self-publishing difficult? Yes. Hard? Yes. Is it impossible? No way.

Self-publishing can be done. It just takes effort, education and a plan.

You're on the right track—in this book you have everything you need to know to get started and be successful in self-publishing. Are you going to find new ways that aren't in the book that work better for you? I'm sure you will. Technology continues to change, and the one thing that is constant in self-publishing is the need to change along with it.

In this book is every tool and tip that I used to sell almost 40,000 books in my first year as an independent publisher. Depending on where you are in your publishing process, you may want to skip around. That's OK...take what you need, when you need it. Remember, self-publishing is all about doing what works best for YOU (and your plan)!

Author as Business Owner

Self-publishing is a brave new world for most people, unlike anything they've ever done in their lives. It certainly was for me! The problem that many of us have is that we are great writers, but terrible business people. In order to be a successful independent author, you will also have to be a good business person, and marketer, and publicist, and so on. Most people don't have backgrounds in all of these specialties, and there is a big learning curve as new authors struggle to figure them out while still trying to write here and there. This book will show you the things you need to know about each facet, so that you still have time to write. After all, you can't be a successful author if you don't have any published books. You're a business person now, and you need to begin thinking like one.

Chapter 3 – The Author as a Business Owner

I'm assuming that you don't have a lot of working capital to start with. That's OK; I didn't either. In fact, when I put $800 on my credit card for my first novel's editing, my wife was aghast. "We don't have that kind of money!" She was right, of course, but I was aware that I knew nothing about writing (I didn't have this book), and I wanted someone to tell me what was wrong with it (quite a lot, as it turned out).

Was the $800 well spent? Yes and no. The editing service I used was the cheapest I could find (by far), and honestly, you get what you pay for. There are many types of editing, and I didn't know the right questions to ask to get what I wanted. For my money, I got advice on writing that was very general in nature, rather than the line editing I expected. Still, I learned an enormous amount that helped me make better decisions later.

As a business owner, you are going to be faced with many decisions on what to spend money on, and what things to do "on the cheap." I will try to give you plenty of ways and times to save money; I will also note when it is IMPERATIVE to fork out some of that hard earned cash as an investment in your future success.

The important point to remember is that you are now not only an author, but a business owner as well, and you are responsible for your brand. When you're making decisions, you need to think about how the outcomes will affect the success or failure of your business over the long term, because this is what we're planning here together, a business that will be successful over the long term. This isn't a get-rich-quick scheme (and you probably won't get rich quick), but if you work hard, you will be successful...and far more successful than you ever would have been working for someone else.

So, you now own a business. What are you going to call it? I called mine "Chris Kennedy Publishing." I wanted everyone to be able to associate me with the brand. While there are some positives with that, if I had it all to do over again, I wouldn't use my name as my business; instead, I would have used something more creative like "High Orbit Publishing" ('Our books take you to outer space!'), or something like that. This is actually my biggest publishing regret, and the one I'd like a "do over" on. At this stage of the game, though, I have a lot invested in the brand and don't want to make the switch. Maybe I will at some point...but not now.

Why don't I recommend using your name? Despite the success of many independent publishers like Hugh Howey, David Gaughran and JA Konrath (and me!), there remains a stigma to independently-published novels. While this is slowly going away, it is easier if you just don't have to fight it. Pick a cool name for your business that is descriptive of the kind of books you want to publish and is something you can be proud of. Sure, I'm proud of my name, but it would have been easier on several occasions to have had a different name for my publishing business. Can you use your name if you want to? Yes. Just be aware that things might go more smoothly if you use something different.

Sooo....you're now a business owner. You need a plan. Don't be scared; I'll be gentle. Depending on how much training you've had in developing business plans, this can be tremendously detailed...or not. It is, however, important to give at least some thought to what you want to do with your new business, where you want it to go and what you hope to achieve. A business plan will keep you organized and give you the guidance required to help attain your goals. As the saying goes, if you don't know where you're going, you're probably never going to get there.

There are as many ways to set up a business plan as there are people to run them. What I'm going to talk about is a very basic, bare-bones approach. I am going to discuss a relatively short time frame (a one-year plan); you should follow the same approach to take a longer look as well (five or ten years, whatever you feel is appropriate) and make sure your short-term plan supports it.

So, where do you start? First, you start by setting goals. In the next year, what would you like to accomplish as a writer? What intermediate goals are going to help get you get there? You should only use goals that are within your power to accomplish. For example, "I'd like to get an agent" is not a good goal as it is not something you can do on your own. If getting an agent is important to you, it would be more appropriate to use "research how to secure an agent" and "query 100 agents" as your goals, as they are specific, measurable and achievable.

What things do you want to achieve? Where do you want to be in a year? How do you want to grow? Write everything you can think of down on a sheet of paper. At a minimum, some areas you'll probably want to explore are your professional goals (like the number of books/articles you want to publish and/or the number of contests you'd like to enter), working on your platform (developing your social media presence, attending conferences and conventions), increasing your marketing (soliciting reviews and branding) and developing yourself as an author (joining a critique group, taking classes and attending workshops).

After you have your list of goals for the next year, read through it and try to find the overarching themes and how important each is to you. Group them so you can see what your biggest themes are. You will probably have many that are related to the areas listed above, but everyone starts out from a different place. Maybe you were already a blogger and have a solid social media presence; in that case, you might not need as much platform development.

Make sure you focus on what you need, not what you want. You may *want* to spend all your time writing so that you can publish four books in the upcoming year (hoping to make some money), but if the books aren't going to be any good because your skills need to be developed, you'd be better off concentrating a healthy portion of your time in that area. Because everyone is different, it is important to take a critical look at yourself. I came from a non-writing background; I knew that continuing to develop my writing skills would be crucial to me keeping an audience beyond my first book. You may have some great story ideas, but if you can't string two sentences together clearly, you're not going to be successful over the long term.

Once you've ranked your goals, pick two or three areas that you're going to focus on over the next year and some supporting goals to pursue. For each of these, develop some action steps that will bring them to completion. For example, if your goal was to "Improve My Writing," you might have the action steps of "Take a class on character development" and "Join the local writers group." Just like the goals, your action steps need to be specific, measurable and achievable. They also shouldn't require more resources (time and/or funding) than you have available.

As a new author, two common focus areas would be to provide new product for your readers and to develop your platform. For the area of providing product, a supporting goal might be to write two books this year. Some action steps to support this goal could be to change your schedule to write 500 words a day and to develop covers for your two books. If done faithfully, writing 500 words a day will give you two 90,000 word novels. For the focus area of developing your platform, some goals to support it might be to create a website (if you don't have one, or improve it if you do), to develop a social media plan and to implement a plan to speak at two conventions to advertise your works.

The bottom line with this process is that it has to work for you, and it has to include items that you can track so you know when you have accomplished them. Once you have completed this process, enter the plan into a spreadsheet or hand write it on a piece of paper, and keep it where you write so that looking at it is a part of your daily routine. As the business owner, it is easy to get side-tracked by unimportant things or feel overwhelmed with how much there is to do (probably more than you can get to, especially if you have a day job like I do). Having a plan allows you to focus on implementing the items that are most important to you and provides a tool to guide your daily efforts.

The key to the plan is not how it looks, but that the plan provides a road map to ensure you accomplish what you want/need to in the coming year. It doesn't have to be anything more than a table or set of lists. For example, Table 1 shows what a basic plan might look like for building your initial author platform. Other areas, like developing product (you have to write!) and professional development could also be included.

Business Plan for 2016			
Focus Area	**Goal**	**Timing**	**Action Steps**
Develop Author Platform	Implement Website	January – February	• Research hosting companies and options • Design site content • Implement email capture program
	Implement Social Media Sites	February – March and then ongoing	• Determine which sites fit my style • Implement 2 sites on social media • Grow selected sites to 500 members
	Develop Amazon Author Central Site	February – March	• Populate Author Central website • Ensure all books are tied in • Connect to social media

Table 1. Business Plan Model

Chapter 4 – Getting Started with Crowd Funding

Depending on your finances, you might need additional capital to get your project off the ground, so I am including a short chapter on crowd funding. What is crowd funding? It's where people make appeals for help with financing various endeavors and give their benefactors gifts based on their levels of patronage. If enough people donate to the project, it moves forward. The first crowd funding site to gain prominence was Kickstarter, but many other crowd funding sites have emerged, including sites that target specific markets. One of these is Pubslush, which focuses on literary projects. Most of the other crowd funding sites are similar in function.

How does Pubslush work? It's not that difficult. After you log onto the site (http://pubslush.com/) and create an account, the site walks you through the process of entering all of the required information. The hardest part of crowd funding is getting people excited about the campaign once it starts (just like any other fundraising effort). The two keys to setting up a successful campaign are to (1) set a reasonable goal and (2) create good rewards.

As far as the goal goes, more people will be willing to get behind a project if it has a reasonable goal tied to sensible expenses. Most people would see donations for editing and cover design as realistic expenses. Lunches at a five-star restaurant to "get you in the mood to write" would probably not win much support.

One of the best ways to get assistance is to include goodies to help win donors' support. They could be anything from autographed copies of the book (at lower levels of support) on up to bigger and better prizes at higher levels. You are only limited by your creativity. You could include donors' names in future books, give them input on future books, do promotions for donors' goods/services on your social media sites or offer your own services for them (proof-reading, editing, etc.).

What else can you do to ensure success? Spread the word as widely as possible through your social media sites and continue to do so throughout the promotion. Make sure you keep your supporters (both donors and potential donors) updated on the project's status throughout the process. If you get close, people might jump in at the end to push you over the limit. One of the most important things you can do is to have a video of yourself talking about the project. The human touch is the best way to reach people, as a Davidson found that campaigns are 85% more likely to be successful if the author uses a video to talk about the project.

Me? A Marketer?

I'm sure that most of you are ready to talk about writing a great story or designing a cover that is going to knock your readers' socks off, but we need to talk about marketing first. Why's that? Because your marketing efforts need to begin prior to the launch of your book. Some people say that six months prior to the book's release is the right time to start, although others note that it's hard to market something without actually having the product to show. While six months might be a little long, I can tell you for sure that if you wait until your book comes out to start marketing, you have waited far too long. You are going to have a tremendously hard time developing any "buzz" about your book unless you start marketing early! However, if you're like I was, you may not have had a lot of education or practical experience in marketing, so you may not know where to start. You've been a consumer all of your life, though, and you know what you like and don't like. That's all that marketing is—presenting your product in a way that makes it pleasing to a customer, along with a "call to action" that gets them to make the purchase. Relationships are at the heart of marketing, just like they are at the heart of everything else in life. The central part of your marketing efforts will be the creation of your author platform, as that's where the relationship will start.

Chapter 5 – Creating Your Author Platform

What's your author platform? It's all of your online "stuff" that builds a picture of you for your adoring fans. It's what lets your readers get to know you and helps them build an emotional connection to you. It shows your readers who you are, what you do, and most importantly, why you do it.

Another way to look at this (in marketing terms) is that you are developing your brand. I'm sure you're saying, "First I've got to develop a platform and now a brand? This is getting too hard!" Stay with me; it's not that bad. <u>You</u> are your brand. It's how you appear in public, as well as the expectations your readers have about connecting with you. When you post on Facebook, what are you like? Do you help and educate your readers, or do you make fun of them? Your public persona is what your readers are going to use to make decisions on whether to do business with you (or not).

Here's who I am. I am an author who writes science fiction and fantasy. I try to be humorous, helpful and friendly in all of my dealings with readers, whether that occurs in my books, through online social media or in person at author events or conventions. On Twitter (<u>@ChrisKennedy110</u>), I tweet about articles that educate developing authors or in-form them about current events in the publishing industry. The talks I do at conventions also educate budding authors on how to become successful independent authors. Want to get your name in an upcoming book? Visit my website and sign up to be a Red Shirt. Sure, you're not going to make it out of the story alive, but at least you'll see your name in print and go out in a blaze of glory. My brand is consistent, using the same picture on all of my social media sites; I'm the same person everywhere, regardless of where you find me.

Why is this level of consistency important? Because you are working to establish a link to your readers. At a basic level, you are selling your personality. If readers like you and can relate to you, they are more likely to purchase your books. They will want to learn more about you and will start to follow you. When you post something on your social media sites, they are more likely to pass it on, and your message will get out to a far larger audience than you would have been able to connect with on your own. Even more importantly, when you launch a new book, they are going to be right there to purchase it, driving up sales to where you get on Amazon's marketing lists (more on this later). Why are they going to do all of this for you? Because you'll have an emotional connection with them. Unfortunately, this takes time.

Where most authors go wrong is they wait until they publish their book to start their marketing efforts, and then they try to push their book without having any sort of relationship with their readers. Without this connection, readers will ignore your posts and have no desire to purchase your book. The goal of your marketing and branding efforts is to bring people either to Amazon or your website ready to purchase your book. When they get there, they'll find a great book waiting for them, with a great cover and sales description, and they will be ready to buy. If they reach these sites without any knowledge of who you are and what you're about, at least you will have your picture and author bio there to make an initial connection.

Speaking of your biography, what should it say? Many people don't like talking about themselves, but your bio is key to letting your potential customers know who you are so they can establish a link to you. You do so by developing an emotional story that draws your potential customers in. How do you do that? You do that by telling readers who you are, why you're writing and who you are writing for. None of your readers care about most of the things in your past; they care about who you are *right now*. It doesn't have to be flashy, and it shouldn't come across as bragging. If you have two big dogs, love chocolate and despise doing anything that is even vaguely math-related, feel free to tell your readers that. You want to sound like you're human and someone that they can empathize with.

Now that you know who you are, you need to decide how you want to be known as a writer. What are you going to write? How are you going to write it? What about you stands out? Many authors want to be known as the expert or source for some type of information and will market themselves as such, like "The Source for Blogging Info" or "The Cover Expert." Perhaps you want to write a series of books on a certain topic or theme (like Jack Canfield's "Chicken Soup" series).

It's important that you develop something that is unique and stands out from the crowd. Remember, there are *hundreds of thousands* of new books on Amazon every year, and you need to give readers a reason to pick your book over the others in your genre. What makes your book special? Is it a new perspective on an old topic? A new location that no one has ever read about? Perhaps it combines different themes in a new manner. My tag line shows that you can expect a cross-genre read with my books; they are "Science Fiction...With a Side of Fantasy."

One final word on branding is "consistency;" you should use the same branding (title, tag line, photo and colors, etc.) across all of your social networks. The more books you write with these themes or elements in place, and the more consistent your message across all of your social media sites, the stronger your brand becomes and the more books you will sell.

Chapter 6 – 5 Places You Have to Be; 5 Things You Have to Do

Okay, so you know what you want to say about yourself. How and where are you going to say it? Social media. Why there? The price is right, as most sites are free. The only thing it costs is your time (which is a valuable commodity; never forget that!). Compared to traditional marketing, social media is a tremendously powerful choice in terms of return on investment.

The biggest issues with social media are choosing which sites to use and limiting your time on them (especially Facebook, which can be a tremendous time vampire).

For an author just starting out, there are five places that you *have* to be. Can you do more than these? Absolutely, but spreading yourself too thin comes at a price; you are an author and need to be spending time writing (it's what actually earns you money). Burnout is one of the top reasons that authors stop marketing their books. They start out with lofty goals of how much time they will devote to their marketing pursuits but then find out they can't routinely maintain these levels. When they find out they can't accomplish what they intended, they get frustrated and quit marketing, which is the death of their book.

How much time do you need to spend? I've seen a number of blogs recommend authors use 70% of their available time for creative writing and 30% for promotion. I think this is an appropriate ratio, as I use close to this for my own work. I usually spend at least 30 minutes twice a day in marketing pursuits; I spend 30 minutes in the morning on Twitter, and then 30 minutes in the evening responding to emails or social media posts. What if you don't have an hour for marketing? If you can devote even 15 minutes daily, and you can keep it up consistently year-round, you'll be able to keep your "buzz" going. Anything else you do is gravy.

So...what are the five places you need to be? First, regardless of whether you blog or not, you HAVE to have a website. It is the heart of your new media empire. We'll talk about it more in the next chapter, but for now, just accept that you must have a website.

After that, you need to have one or two social media sites that you can keep up with. Why just one or two sites when you have so many opportunities? You don't want to spread yourself too thin, which is easy to do. I would recommend that one of your sites be Facebook (www.facebook.com), as it is pretty much an industry-wide expectation that an author will have a Facebook site, and it is a great place for putting out information. If a fan "likes" your page, they will see your posts in their feed (assuming that they look at it periodically; Facebook continues to try to guess what you want to see and is becoming more and more selective of what it shows). Whether you use your personal site or start an author site is up to you. If you want to create an author's page, use the "Create a Page for a celebrity, band or business" option.

There are a number of other sites that an author can be active on; Twitter (www.twitter.com) is probably the second most popular. Like Facebook, it lets you disseminate information to your followers. More importantly, it also lets you follow sources of information that could be valuable to you. For example, I follow several people that post great information daily; this keeps me current on industry news and helps me continue to develop myself. When I see articles that I'm interested in, I click over and read them.

If Twitter isn't "your thing" there are a number of other social media sites to help you reach your followers. The fastest growing is Pinterest (www.pinterest.com), which lets you post pictures and interact through them. Chrzan notes that over 83% of the people on Pinterest are women, so that is a great site to use if your target audience is female.

The fourth site to be on is Amazon's Author Central (https://authorcentral.amazon.com). I'm amazed at how many authors don't fill out their Author Central profile. This is an easy way to reach your readers when they're making purchasing decisions on Amazon (which will probably be your largest retailer, by a long shot), and to let them know about other books or products you have. In addition, I usually look to see what authors have to say. When I find that their Author Central profiles are blank or nonexistent, I usually decide they aren't serious authors and look for something else to buy.

The fifth site is Goodreads (www.goodreads.com). It's easy to put your profile on the site so people can learn more about you. Goodreads also has a number of promotions you can use to market your book if you would like. It's free, easy and doesn't take any time to maintain. Why wouldn't you want to use it? The only potential drawback to the site is that it has been my experience that the readers are more discerning (and far more critical in their reviews) on Goodreads than on Amazon. When you get good reviews there, you know that you're really doing well!

So, you're now on all of these sites. Most authors will already be familiar with "netiquette" (net etiquette), but as a reminder, there are a few guidelines that will serve you well across all of them. First, remember to be kind and genuine to your followers and to show gratitude for everything they do for you. Without them, you are nothing; treat them like gold for following you and/or liking your pages.

An outgrowth of the first guideline, the second is to acknowledge comments from others. Social media is a two-way street; both parties get the most out of the relationship when it *is* a relationship. Two-way communications are necessary for that to occur. Make sure you "like" readers' posts, answer their questions and engage with them.

Third, don't be boring, cold and distant; spice up your posts with fun information about yourself and use pictures whenever you can! Engagement levels almost always increase when people use visual content in their posts.

Fourth, know what to keep in and what to leave out. Humor done well (that doesn't target your audience) is great for increasing engagement. Stay away from politics and religion, as you will lose at least half of your audience, no matter what you post.

Finally, accept the fact that your social media platform is your responsibility. No one will do it as well as you. The only way that you remain true to your audience is if you are the one who interacts with them. Having someone else manage your social media sites opens you up to being misconstrued when he or she says something different than what you really think or feel. Worse, once it's been said, it's hard to call back.

Chapter 7 – The Blog/Website

The heart of your social media marketing campaign is your website or blog, which is going to draw your readers in and capture their information. How are you going to do that? One way to get people to your website is to put your web address on all of your promotional material. It will be everywhere, inescapable, to the point that readers finally go to it just to see what you have.

And then you've got them because you will have information (content) on your website that captures their attention as well as their email address (as long as they opt in). Don't just try to sell them, incorporate other information that reflects their interests. In the course of your posts, it's fine to talk about your other books and the things you do; adding other content will make the website less "pitchy," so that when they come to sales info, your readers will be more open to it.

Wait? You don't know how to start a website? Don't worry, we'll get to that shortly.

Why do you want your readers' email addresses? Because it allows you to notify all of them, at any given moment, when your next book is published, or when any other promotions are going on. It's instant access (or nearly so, these days) to the people that like what you do. Email is also a stronger marketing link than social media advertising. You don't just "want" email addresses; you "need" email addresses. If you don't have a database of fans, you need to have a plan to gather email addresses on your website and at any events you participate in (for example, having a sheet for people to write down their information on the promise that you'll email them a chapter of your next book).

Your website should have an easily recognizable domain name so readers and the media can find you. Additionally, if you brand yourself with a tag line or expert status, you may want to purchase that domain name and redirect to it as well. The name of your site and its tag line should make it easy for viewers to tell what you are about.

How do you get people to find your website? One way is to post intriguing teasers about your blog posts, or what you're doing on your other social media sites. The key is to be interesting; if all you do is say "Buy my books," people will rapidly tune out (and not come back). But, if you promise a free chapter of your latest novel if they visit your website, they are much more likely to visit. People are on social media to be entertained, not to be "sold." It's okay to have a limited number of promotional tweets embedded among interesting content; when the promotional material becomes the main thrust, it's a problem.

So, how do you set up a site? It's not hard.

Chapter 8 – How to Create a WordPress Blog

Why would you want to use WordPress to run your website? Because it's the most popular content management system in use on the internet. According to Mullenweg, Version 3.3 was downloaded over 65 million times; the current version (4.1) has already been downloaded over 10 million times (https://wordpress.org/download/counter/). Most blogs and websites these days use the WordPress platform because it's easy to set up and maintain, and it provides the flexibility and personalization necessary to customize it to your needs. You only need two things to start a website, hosting and your domain name.

The first thing you need to do is choose your web host, the company that is going to provide the hosting for your site. There are a large number of hosting companies available, but if you are using WordPress, you should probably consider Bluehost (http://www.bluehost.com/). Warnock notes that it is the only hosting service officially recommended by WordPress (which it has been for almost 10 years). I use Bluehost and have found it to have great customer service, reliability and an easy-to-use control panel. They often run specials where you can get hosting for $3.95/month, as well as a free domain name for a year.

Getting started with Bluehost is easy, just go to their website and click on the "Get Started Now" button. You will be presented with several options. Pick the one that works for you and click on "Select." Next, choose the domain name for your site. If you already have one, you can enter it in the "I Already Have One" box; otherwise, you can select one in the "New Domain" box. Once you've entered a domain name, fill in your personal information.

The next step is to choose which hosting package you want. Shared hosting (where many organizations' websites will be resident on the same web server) is priced in 12, 24 and 36-month blocks. The longer block you purchase, the lower the monthly rate. If you choose Bluehost, they will provide a seamless upgrade if you ever need more than a shared hosting account. There are a few other offers provided at sign up, which you can include at your discretion. One I would recommend is Domain Privacy, a paid service that keeps your personal information private. Should you decide you want them, Site Backup and Domain Security are also good investments for protecting your website.

After you've made your selections and filled in the billing information, click the "Next" button to complete your purchase. You'll then be asked to create a password for your account. You can use either use the Password Generator or create one yourself, but the system requires that you have both capital and lowercase letters, a number and a special character so that your account is well-protected.

You are now signed up and able to log into your account; it's time to install WordPress! This will probably seem like the most complicated step, but Bluehost has made it easier by implementing its MOJO Marketplace for installing WordPress and other applications. In the cPanel (Bluehost's control panel), go to the section titled "MOJO Marketplace" and select the "One-Click Installs" button, which will take you to a page called "Script Installs." The blog section is at the top of the page; click on the WordPress icon, and it will open the installation window. Clicking on the green "Start" button will start the WordPress installation process. Three steps to go.

First, you need to choose where you want to install WordPress. It can be on any domain on your account, or a subdomain or a folder for one of your domains. Click on "Check Domain," which will make sure the domain is assigned and pointing to your account. You may get a warning that you are overwriting files, but as long as you don't have another website built, you can check the box and continue. If you do have other sites built, make sure you're not overwriting something important.

Second, complete the "show advanced options" section, which lets you set up your username and password for your WordPress install. PLEASE use a different username than "admin" and a very strong password. If you use the "admin" username, hackers can perform a brute force attack to crack your login and take control of your site. Since WordPress gives you the option to change the username, it doesn't make sense to keep the default one. Make sure that the "Automatically create a new database for this installation" box is checked, unless you have a database already set up.

Finally, read the terms and conditions. If you agree with them, you can check the box and click "Install Now." You will see the progress page, which shows how far along the installation is. Once WordPress is installed, it will provide you with your site URL, the admin login URL, your username, and password. You will also get a copy of this information (except your password) in your email. Keep it in a safe place!

Now you can visit your WordPress site by going to the admin login URL and entering your login information, which will take you to your WordPress dashboard. From there, you can control everything to do with your WordPress site, such as adding pages, writing posts and changing the appearance.

Chapter 9 – Why You Should Blog

Now that you've gone through the trouble of implementing a website, you're going to want to use it, right? One of the best things you can do is to implement a blog, because a blog that delivers good content will help you cultivate your platform, as well as give you opportunities to practice your craft and find your voice.

But, really, *why* do you want to blog? To get noticed. Ideally by your readers, but also by your colleagues, peers and the media...and by Google, too! The three most important communities that you want to tie into are 1) readers who will purchase your books, 2) supporters who will spread the word about your books, and 3) other authors and editors who will help you develop your craft and business.

As you start to look at who your audience is, and what content you are going to provide, try to keep some scalability in mind. What's scalability? The ability to reuse information. The ideal blog helps you develop material you can use again (and again). Can portions of your blog be used on your Twitter and Facebook feeds to drive traffic to your website? If you plan far enough in advance, you can also string enough posts together to create a body of work you can sell or utilize as another marketing tool. Depending on your topic, individual posts might be edited into a variety of things, from a cookbook, to an anthology, to a travel guide. You can sell these in their entirety, as well as use portions of them as giveaways and incentives for people to subscribe to your blog. One thing to note before you start is search engines don't like duplicate content; don't republish exact posts on other websites.

The important thing about content is it must deliver value. People want entertainment and information. They want to know things that will help them lead better lives, become more successful or help them avoid potential problems. Your posts don't have to be long or complicated; in fact, some of the most popular posts are lists of "how-to" or "best/worst." These are also great for repurposing; after a few months you'll have enough chapters for a book!

Chapter 10 – 8 Things Not to Do on Your Blog

Just like there were rules for netiquette, there are also rules for what you should and shouldn't do on your blog. Here are eight rules the beginning blogger violates at his or her own peril:

1. **Don't use cute, clever or confusing headlines.** Your headline is going to appear in a number of places, and you want it to draw readers *into* your post, not push them away. You do that with headlines that are unique, ultra-specific, useful or urgent (or even better, a combination of these things). Here are a few examples:

- 5 Lessons You Can Learn from the Fall of MySpace (Unique)
- 20 Ways to Become a Pinterest Power User (Ultra-Specific)
- How to Get Your Book Onto Bestseller Lists (Useful)
- 10 Things to Remove from Your Diet Before They Kill You! (Urgent)

2. **Don't use an inappropriate or defective Word-Press background (the WordPress "theme.")** The right Wordpress theme, or background that you use, can help your site grow and prosper; the wrong one can be a tremendous detriment. Regardless of whether you use a stock theme included with WordPress or purchase one from

another vendor, you want one that is easy for you to use and looks good with your material.

3. **Don't forget to change the default tagline of "just another blog."** WordPress adds that tagline to every installation, and nothing says "newbie" to a reader like seeing that at the top of your website. Your website's tagline should say something about you and/or the site. It's easy to change, just go to Settings >> General in your WordPress dashboard. While you're there, make sure you delete the sample page that came with your WordPress install, too.

4. **Don't use WordPress' default permalink structure.** What's a permalink? It's an unchanging hyperlink to a post on your site. Usually, WordPress uses a default structure that looks like: www.yoursite.com/?p=123. A search-engine friendly permalink structure that describes the page will help you improve your search engine ranking, help users find you and will show your readers you're a professional. How do you change this? Go to Settings » Permalinks. Once you've changed it, you can increase your search engine optimization by using applicable keywords in your permalink structure.

5. **Don't forget to put an email capture form on your site.** A common mistake (and one I was guilty of for far too long) is not to have some way of capturing visitors' email addresses. These are gold! Let me repeat, you need an email capture form! Two that are especially good are Mail-Chimp and AWeber (I use AWeber: https://www.aweber.com/). Both of these will also keep you within the federal anti-spam guidelines by requiring readers opt in to be part of your list. Offer something of value to your readers if they join your mailing list, like a free short

story or an advance chapter of your next book. There's no telling how many sales I missed because I let hundreds of potential customers escape me, but I'm sure it was plenty. Don't let this happen to you!

6. **Don't forget to create a backup.** One of the biggest mistakes authors make is not backing up our websites. We all know we should...but then we wait until disaster strikes to get around to it. Make sure you backup your WordPress site, especially if you're installing an update. It's easy! All you have to do is go to Tools >> Export on your dashboard, and you can generate a backup file that can be used to recover from a crash or hack.

7. **Don't ignore WordPress updates.** The WordPress developers are always working to make the program as safe as possible and improve its speed and usability. Whenever they find a new bug or vulnerability, they update the core program. When you see a new update, make sure you download it as soon as possible. It's an easy process that makes your site more secure; just follow the prompts when they appear.

8. **Don't forget to ask readers to leave comments.** A post all by itself seems to lack credibility; however, it is often difficult to get people to take the time to leave a comment. One way to get your readers to leave comments is to ask for them. At the end of every post, put a simple question related to your post that begs an answer. If your post was about ways to optimize your WordPress site, you might end your post with, "What other ways have you found to optimize your WordPress site?" or "What is the best tip you have found?"

If you are writing detailed posts, you are more likely to get comments, especially if there are other areas that weren't covered or need more explanation. That's okay; you want comments because it's proof people are reading what you're writing and think it's valuable. The comments are social media in action.

Chapter 11 – Facebook and Engagement

Although there are many up-and-coming social media sites, Facebook continues to be first and foremost, and a place where you need to be. It's expected. After your blog/website, it will be the most visited site in your burgeoning social media empire. Why should you care about Facebook, especially if you're like me and never had a Facebook page prior to your career as an author? It's all about making those connections, and it's all about engagement.

What's engagement? It's the interaction that occurs with a visitor on your site, and can be anything from "liking" the site, to posting a link or photo, to entering into a conversation with you. What stimulates readers' engagement? Usually, it's what you post; the content you put on the site will draw them in and involve them (or it won't). What should you post and when? Cooper noted five points.

First, this will probably come as no surprise, but people like winning things and getting in on deals. If you are advertising a promotion you're running, you are likely to engage readers that find your site. It doesn't seem to matter whether it is a contest, a coupon or a discount; people like to get things (especially for free).

Keep it simple. Readers tend to be more engaged when your posts are short. Facebook posts fewer than 80 characters have higher engagement rates than those that are longer. Keeping your posts concise will lead to greater engagement.

Timing your posts helps engagement, too. People that are off work are more likely to have time to stop and read your posts than those just skimming the internet at work. The research agrees, showing a much higher engagement rate after normal business hours. In fact, 8:00 p.m. is the best time for posting on Facebook.

Want more engagement? Video and images are great for increasing engagement, as long as you don't use URL shorteners on your links. A URL shortener is used to take a long web address and shorten it, so that it is easier to use or takes up less space. Unfortunately, when you shorten the URL, the readers lose any information they might have received. Having the full link makes it easier for people to trust the link and click on it.

One last way to get participation is to be inclusive. Want participation? Ask for it. Ask people to "Like" your posts, "Tell Us" what they think about them and "Post" their own "Comments."

Chapter 12 – Navigating Twitter

One of the biggest social media sites currently in use is Twitter, even though it requires you to send the shortest messages. 140 characters are all you get. That's not a lot of copy to get people to follow you, and if they aren't following you, they aren't getting your message. Worse, they're not sharing it with their followers, which is the power of Twitter. There's nothing quite like sending out a message to several thousand followers, and then watching it get turned around to several *hundred thousand* others! The challenge is in getting the first people to follow you. How is that done? It isn't hard; it just takes a little time and effort on your part.

There are a number of ways to get people to follow you on Twitter. The first and easiest is to follow other people, as a good portion of them will follow you back. This will begin the cascade effect; now that they can see your tweets, they may find them valuable and share them with their followers ("retweet" them). This will also bring new people to your banner.

Who else should you follow? The best thing to do is to start following the people that are most interested in the things you tweet about. For example, if you tweet about self-publishing, some obvious Twitter accounts would be those people that are either independent authors or readers. Expanding the circle a little, you could also include people that blog about books, people who review books, and literary magazines. From there you could get into additional industries that support them. Of course, there are tens of thousands of authors on Twitter alone, so it will take you a while just to work your way through them!

Other people to follow are those who are similar to you. Using the self-publishing example from above, other good people to follow would be independent publishers and traditional publishers. They may well have information important to you or advice you need; by following them, you keep up with your own industry. You can also follow the people who follow accounts similar to yours. If they are customers of publishers or care about what publishers say, you want them to listen to you, too. Once you have them, don't stop there; look to see who they're following. Not only are you going to discover new accounts to follow, but you're also going to learn more about your industry and find other people who may want to follow you back.

A special sub-group of this last group are the topical leaders in your industry. While these people may not follow you back (they probably won't), they are people consumers and other producers in your industry listen to. They probably have information you need to know, so they are worth following. Once again, check out the people who are following them; they are likely to follow you back.

This search strategy should identify many accounts worth following, but you don't want to try to follow *everyone* at the start. There are two reasons why. First, if you are following a lot of people, but no one is following you, you don't appear to be worth following (you look needy), so people are less likely to follow you back. Yes, it's almost like being in high school all over again, but at least this time you have some say in it. By keeping the number of people you follow fairly close to the number of followers you have, you give the appearance you are someone worth following. Second, this will help as you get to the 2,000 person Twitter limit. Up to this number, you can follow as many people as you want. Once you exceed it, though, you can't follow any more accounts until your ratio of followers to following is within an acceptable range. What's the ratio? No one knows; Twitter doesn't make that figure public.

What happens if you follow a bunch of people, and they don't follow you back? Don't get upset about it; if they haven't followed you back within a week or so, just unfollow them and follow someone else. The web service Just Unfollow (https://www.justunfollow.com) makes it very easy to see who isn't following you...and to give them the axe. You might want to keep some industry leaders or content providers who will never follow you back, but for the rest of them, the axe is the way to go.

By now you should have a good group of people to follow; it's also important to know who you don't want to follow (even if they follow you). Generally, you don't want to follow people who are only on Twitter for themselves, such as people who promise you thousands of followers for $5, who never interact with others and who only tweet self-promotional links. They aren't worth following. Axe!

So, now that you have a following (and are spending a few minutes every day building it), what do you do on Twitter? Blast out the link to your book every five minutes so no one will miss it?

NO!

As discussed above, if you do that, you will have just marked yourself as someone who isn't worth following. Remember, this is "social" media, so you need to be social, which involves including others. How do you do that? Engage with others. If you see something interesting or informational, retweet it to your followers. Also, reply to the people that send tweets to you. Yes, this will take time, but it will be paid back. It's okay to send out promotional tweets, but make sure that they aren't more than one out of every four (i.e., send out at least three "content" tweets before you send out one trumpeting your product). This doesn't mean you shouldn't talk about things going on in your life, like the book launches and author events you're attending, just remember to balance them with other items of value to your followers.

Besides spamming (always sending out promotional tweets for your products), there are a few other things to keep in mind as you start out. First, if you are trying to build a following, you probably don't want to use a validation service, as it puts an extra step into the process of following you, which will annoy a lot of people (and keep them from following you). Another service to avoid is the kind that automatically direct-messages people. Most don't like being direct-messaged by a computer, and they will unfollow you. Finally, don't protect your tweets. You want them to be read and shared; this helps build your platform. Protecting them only keeps new people from reading them.

Lastly, have fun. Twitter is social media—use it to learn about your business and make friends.

Chapter 13 – Using Pinterest to Promote Your Business

What's the fastest growing social media site? If you looked at the chapter title, you probably guessed "Pinterest," and you would be right. Author agent Rachelle Gardner noted on her blog that Pinterest had grown over 2,700% in the last ten months and continues to gain market share. Pictures can be very engaging, and Pinterest bears this out. It is the third most engaging site, ranking after Facebook and Tumblr, but ahead of LinkedIn and Google Plus. As was mentioned, though, its demographics are skewed, with women making up a large majority of its users. This may make it more valuable to some authors (like romance novelists) than it is to others.

What's Pinterest all about? It's about sharing photos that users find online by "pinning" them, similar to "liking" something on Facebook. After a user pins it, the photo (and any associated information) shows up on the user's Pinterest board, where it can be seen by any of the user's followers, who can then re-pin it if they want. Including marketing information is more difficult on Pinterest than most of the other sites, but there are ways Pinterest can be used to promote your business and your books...you just need to be a little more creative.

The first (and least creative) method is to share your business by pinning photos of your books or other products. The best way to do this is by grouping photos based on individual themes and creating categories of photos for specific groups of customers (romance readers, mystery buffs, etc.).

This may be especially helpful if you offer added value to your customers by including other products and services that complement your own.

Do you provide services in addition to selling your books and other products? Pinterest can be a great tool for promoting this aspect of your business. This works particularly well if your other services are visual in nature, like web design or photography services. If they aren't, you can pin photos that represent your customers' needs and desires.

Another way to develop interest in your site is to offer exclusive content. Got a discount or promotion? Making it exclusive to your site will draw readers. One romance writer I know posts a new picture of her book's hero each week. The hero is dressed differently every time, and she has started a "What will he be wearing this week?" page for her readers, a large number of whom log in every week to see the new outfit. You're only bound by your imagination, so be creative!

The thing to remember is that Pinterest is a social network, and you need to build relationships with your readers and other patrons. By interacting with them, you form a community that supports each other. Just like any other social media site, thank followers for re-pinning your photos and follow other people who follow you. The more interaction you have with your customers, the better the relationship will be for both of you.

UNIT 4

Writing a Spectacular Book

If 81 percent of the people in the U.S. want to write a book, as estimated by Epstein, why do only one or two percent actually do it? Usually, it is due to one of two reasons: either they don't have a strong enough desire to take the necessary action, or they lack some of the skills necessary to complete the process (and decide becoming an author is beyond them). Since you paid for this book and are reading it, you probably have the desire to write a book. If so, perhaps you feel your writing isn't good enough. You may have even been told *you're* not good enough, and you can't do it. I'm here to tell you, everyone has a first book, and *none* of them are perfect.

You may even feel like I did when I was getting ready to publish my first book. Who was I to think I had anything worth selling? I had never written a book, and there were plenty of good reasons why I shouldn't publish *Red Tide*. I did, though, and you can publish your book, too. Don't think you're good enough? In the editing process of my first book I found out that I had made most of the mistakes common to new writers. This unit documents all of the issues from my first round of edits, so that you don't have to make those same mistakes (you will have to find your own ones!). This section isn't meant to make you an expert prose crafter; only practice can do that. This unit will, however, help you write a story that doesn't look like it's the first time you ever put ink to paper.

One last note before we start. If you're comfortable using Microsoft Word, use that to write your book. There are other software programs for authors you can buy, but it isn't necessary for you to purchase one of them. All of the ebook retailers have conversion programs that will turn Word into the correct digital format. As each of these is slightly different, you'll just need to make a few formatting changes when you're done. The best way to avoid major problems later is to get Amazon's free book, "Building your book for Kindle," http://www.amazon.com/dp/B007URVZJ6, and use it to correctly set up your formatting from the start.

Now let's get down to writing that book.

Chapter 14 – What Should You Be Writing?

So, what should you write about? Vampires are a hot topic right now. Shouldn't you write a book about them to cash in on the craze? Or was that zombies? Wait, that just changed, too. Post-apocalyptic/dystopian is the way to go now, right? How's a writer to keep up with the ever-changing trends?

The best story tellers know their audiences. The best writers do, too, and the things you write about are as important to your success as how you write them. If there is no market for a book, or only a limited audience, it's unlikely you'll sell many copies. The three biggest genres are romance, mystery/thriller and science fiction/fantasy. If you write in one of these areas, you have the ability to reach higher sales than in other areas where there isn't as great a demand. You *can* still write in other areas if that is what you feel you need to do; however, you will need to temper your vision of the level of sales a "successful" book is likely to have.

It's also important to know where you fit within inside a genre, so readers can target your book. The more narrowly you focus, the more successful you are likely to be, as most readers look for a very specific type of book. I don't just write science fiction; I write Space Opera science fiction. Your book shouldn't just be romance, but romantic suspense (or whatever genre you choose). If you target more of a niche, you will be more likely to get a group from the niche to talk about it (and word of mouth is the best advertising).

The bottom line is you shouldn't write a book and then try to market it; you should write a book knowing that it's marketable. If you're in the business to make money, that isn't "selling out" (unless you mean, "selling out your first five print runs"), but writing where there's a market.

Having targeted your market, you also need to start with the end in mind. Most of the advice I heard was to "just write your story." Maybe that works sometimes, but other times you need to know where you are trying to go. I "just wrote" my first book and ended up with an 85,000 word novel. That was wonderful, but then I found out the company I wanted to market it to only accepted books that were at least 100,000 words long. Had I begun with that in mind, I would have written the story differently. If you have a specific goal for your story once it's done, begin with the final product in mind and save yourself some wailing and gnashing of teeth.

A good place to start is to write about what you know and are passionate about, as these two points are more often than not prerequisites for a good story. If you write about something you are interested in, it will likely be a story that you enjoy, and you are more likely to dedicate yourself to it. Not only will you have more fun writing the book, you're also more likely to end up with a better book.

Now that you have your story, let's get that crucial first chapter done.

Chapter 15 – The First Chapter

The first chapter is going to catch and keep your readers, so it's important you get it right. It's going to let readers know what to expect from the book and hook them in to find out more. Don't drive them away with useless information or the same old clichés. There are a number of things to craft into your first chapter, and there are others you will want to make sure you leave out.

First, your book needs to have a good plot and, for fiction books, there needs to be conflict in the first chapter that reaches out and grabs your readers. Something happens to your protagonist that upsets the balance. It spurs your main character on, and readers want to find out what happens. They're hooked!

In addition to plot/conflict, it's important for readers to develop an emotional connection with your main character. If people don't care about your hero, they're going to put your book down and forget about it. Try to show the readers what's going on through the use of body language, emotions and strong dialogue; don't just tell them about it with long descriptions and back story. The seasoned author knows you don't have to tell the reader everything from the start; in fact, it's better if you don't. A little bit of mystery is not only okay, it's great. It makes your readers ask questions, drawing them into the story.

Speaking of the story, the first chapter needs to orient the reader to what is going on. Many times, this is best accomplished by starting a little before the main action begins so the reader gets acclimated to the story, the main character and a couple of the major players before the conflict kicks in. In addition to acclimating the reader to the story, the first chapter also gets readers used to the narrator and the mood and tone of the book, letting them know whether they should expect humor, something dark, or a book that lies somewhere in between.

Does your first chapter have these things? If so, you are well on your way to success. There are, however, some things best left out, as they will bore readers if they're addressed too quickly. As noted above, a large amount of back story is at the top of this list (and will be discussed further in Chapter 17). Also, while it's great to set the scene and describe it to your readers, too much description at the start can be boring. Clear and concise is the way to go. Finally, avoid clichés like "it was a dark and stormy night!" Be fresh; stay away from things that have been done many times previously.

Chapter 16 – How Not to Look Like a Newbie

There are a number of things beginning authors do that make it easy for readers (and experienced authors) to tell this is their first effort. Doing these things doesn't make you a bad writer, per se; it just means that you're human, as most people make these mistakes when they start out.

First, as a professional author, words are your tools, and spelling and grammar count. In today's electronic age, you look lazy when they aren't right. Start out with the automatic spelling and grammar checks and go on from there. Don't know the difference between lie and lay? There are plenty of resources available online to help you, and a hard copy style guide is a worthwhile investment. Use them! Nobody is going to go easy on you just because it's your first book.

Second, get rid of extraneous dialogue tags. "Said" is almost invisible to readers and they skip right over it; when you get too cute with other tags, it pulls the reader out of the story. Anything other than "said" should be used sparingly. That isn't to say that those tags should be avoided entirely, as it is much worse to use an adverb at the end of a dialogue tag than a strong verb. "He joked" is a much better and stronger tag than "he said jokingly." Dialogue tags other than "said" should be used infrequently; dialogue tags with adverbs should be eliminated in almost every case. And above all, don't think that it's cute when you can make a bad pun like: "I should be dead," John croaked. Just don't do it.

Third, just because you have the world's best vocabulary doesn't mean you have to beat your readers with it. Even though your high school English teacher loved it, most of your readers will not. Too much flowery language is distracting and annoying. The story, and the reader's ability to follow it, are much more important than using words most people don't understand. Don't use 50 words to describe something when 20 will do.

Fourth, as mentioned before, only beginners waste the first ten pages of a story giving readers every piece of back story they are likely to need. Changing from narrative back story to an "As you know, Bob" conversation ("As you know, Bob, the terrorists have been doing this for the last five years...") doesn't make it any better.

Finally, just because people say things in real life doesn't mean they have to talk that way in your book. Normal, run-of-the-mill conversation is boring and should be left out. No one wants to hear, "How are you? I am fine. How are you today? I'm good." If the dialogue or the scene doesn't further the story, delete it.

Chapter 17 – Back Story and How to Weave It

Generally, you shouldn't pass huge chunks of back story to the reader via the narrator. If you give the reader all of the information at once, they will quickly become bored and disengaged. Instead, readers need to receive information as they need it and only as much as they need at the time. This occurs through conversation and actions. If you want to pass a character's back story to the reader, you should do it via a conversation (without the "As you know, Bob"). Often, this means that you will be writing scenes to pass on back story.

For example, if it's important readers know your main character was in the army, you should tell them via events and dialogue in a scene. Perhaps he runs into one of his buddies from the old days, and they reminisce about their time in the service. Telling the reader the character was in the army via the narrator is the wrong way to do it. The more naturally you can pass on back story, the better your story will read.

Why is this? Because back story, by definition, takes the story backward. Regardless of whether it is conducted with dream sequences, character musings or large tracts of prose, every time you add back story, you stop the novel's forward momentum and risk having the reader put the book down to do something else.

Just like you shhouldn't give out too much back story at the start of your novel, you also don't want to give out too much at a time. Besides distracting readers with the extra information, writers who reveal too much take away much of the story's fun. Part of the reading experience is trying to predict what's going to happen; when the author gives the reader too much information too soon, that doesn't happen, and the reader ends up being far less engaged. Back story is often compared with a 'connect-the-dots' picture. The author just needs to write the dots; the reader will draw the lines.

Chapter 18 – Character/Location Description

Stephen King noted in his book, *On Writing*, that the process of writing is like telepathy (97); the author is trying to get the images in his or her mind into the mind of the reader. How is this done? Through the use of character and location description. Although you don't need to over-describe these things, it is important to give the readers enough description that they are able to get a mental picture of both. The reason you don't want to over-describe is that no matter what you say, your words will never be as powerful as the reader's imagination. For example, if you say "a sports car" sped past the main character, it will conjure a certain image in the reader's mind. Saying "a red sports car" will conjure a different image, and "a red Ferrari convertible with its top down" will create a third. The key to good writing is to use just enough words that the reader will be able to paint a better picture than you are describing. How do you do that?

For location, you need a description of the scene every time your characters change locations. If the location is important, the description needs to show it by being more developed. You don't have to give all of the details at once, especially if the character will be returning to the site in the future; it can be layered across scenes.

For minor characters, the amount of description each receives is relative to their importance in the story. The more important the character, the more description is needed. For example, the person standing in front of the character at an ATM might be nothing more than "a young lady in a blue dress."

This rule of thumb also applies to major characters—the more important the character, the more description you need. The more you describe a character, the more a reader will emotionally invest in them; you can indicate which characters are important simply by the amount of description each receives. Just as with important locations, not all of the character description needs to be given at once (and it's usually better if it's not). The description can be layered over a number of chapters or appearances; just start simple and add nuances as the story progresses.

It is important to note one last thing about full character descriptions. As mentioned above, readers will emotionally invest in characters that receive a lot of description. Unless you are George R. R. Martin (or me), readers will not expect a character described in detail to be killed off, and it will often leave them frustrated. Author beware!

Chapter 19 – On Adverbs

Most books on writing will tell you that adverbs are not your friends, and in most cases, that is true. Why? Because they are often used when writers are afraid they aren't expressing themselves clearly, or they're not getting the picture across. Usually, a stronger verb will remove the need for the adverb; as such, your writing is stronger if you find the better verb and get rid of the adverb. This is especially true if you are using adverbs to supplement dialogue tags (which we already decided not to do).

For example, take a look at the sentence, "He drove the car away quickly." It's an okay sentence that has an active voice verb in it, but is there a better way to say it? How about "He sped off down the street," or "He raced out of the parking spot?" The prose that preceded this passage will also help set the scene for how the action occurred, eliminating the need for the adverb.

Just like using dialogue tags other than "said," it isn't always wrong to use adverbs, and there are places where they are justified. The problem is once you start using them, they become habitual, and authors find themselves using them more and more often, while their prose becomes increasingly weaker.

Chapter 20 – Show, Don't Tell

Every author has heard the saying, "Show, don't tell." It is a worn out cliché; however, it is a key concept to good storytelling. "Showing" keeps readers active and involved as they put together the clues left for them. "Telling" readers things keeps them more passive. They sit outside the story watching what is happening, rather than becoming active participants in the process. The best way to show readers is to feed them the back story information via conversation rather than a narrative dump. In most cases, the only things the narrator should be describing are events, characters and conversations. Characters' reactions to events and the words they use are the appropriate methods for delivering back story.

For example, consider the following:

"Dantes and John climbed up the mountain. It was cold and the mountain was tall, so it took them most of the day."

That's telling, with no interaction on the reader's part. Contrast it with the following:

"Geez," said John, his heavy breathing coming out like smoke in the frigid mountain air, "we've been climbing all day."

Dantes paused and looked up to the mountain's peak, wreathed in clouds. "Less talking," he gasped. "If we push on, we can get there before dark."

The bottom line is you want to deliver details via dialogue. Your goal is to paint a picture readers can envision and flesh out in their minds. The more specific you are, the more likely it is you are showing, rather than telling.

Making Your Book Better

Although much improved lately, self-publishing has had a bad reputation in the past due to the quality of its editing (or lack, thereof). In the rush to publish, authors would often skip the editing process, believing 'I read the book twice, what more does it need?' The fact of the matter is, your story needs to be edited. "But I can't afford it!" There are plenty of ways you can get editing done very economically, although the process will take a little bit of effort on your part and may slow down the publishing process a little. Don't bypass editing. Not only will it make you look more like a professional and increase your sales, publishing quality books is also good for self-publishing in general, and it will help all of our sales.

Chapter 21 – On the Editing of Books

Your book needs to be edited. This is a simple statement of fact, regardless of whether you are an experienced author or a writer who is just starting out. Editing is what separates a successful independent writer from those who have given self-publishing a bad name in the past. The human mind is an interesting thing; by the time you've read your book several times, you know what it's supposed to say, and you aren't actually reading the words any more even though your eyes may be going over them.

But what about Microsoft Word's spelling and grammar checker? Isn't that good enough? In a word, no. It's far from perfect as it won't find words that are spelled correctly but are misused, nor will it catch the improper use of homonyms. In my last book, the characters often talked about a prophecy (the noun), but about half of the time I spelled it "prophesy" (which is the verb). Spell check thought that was an okay substitution, but it (obviously) was not. If those errors aren't bad enough, it also sometimes flags words as wrong when they are, in fact, correct.

So, don't use automatic checkers? No, you *should* use spelling and grammar checking software. They are handy tools for catching the majority of errors, and I am not suggesting abandoning them. I know my editors are happier when I use them than when I don't. These tools don't catch needless repetition, uneven pacing and side-plots that go nowhere, however, so they shouldn't be more than the first step in the editing process.

What are the other steps? There are many types of editors you might need to look at your book. Developmental editors help with the structure and argument of a nonfiction book or the plot and character in a work of fiction. A line editor also looks at the whole manuscript, but doesn't edit as deeply. A copy editor looks at the book's language or copy and tries to keep the style clean and consistent throughout. The last people to view your book are the proofreaders, who read it prior to printing and distribution. They check the book for misspellings or errors in style, such as improper punctuation, grammar or formatting.

The problem with editors is they aren't cheap, and using the cheapest ones you can find is probably not the best advice. Just like anything else in life, you get what you pay for, and you should budget what you can to get the help and advice you need. As I discussed above, there are a variety of editors available, and the level of service they provide is directly related to how much they are going to charge. A deep, developmental edit will cost more than proofreading services.

So how do you find the right editor for what you need? The best place to start is to ask your writer friends for recommendations. If that doesn't work, look for local freelance editors you can meet face-to-face. That way, you will be better able to judge them than if you just selected them from an online service. This is especially important if you are going to need them long-term. If you can't find one locally, there are plenty of other place to look, like Elance.com.

Once you develop a list of candidates, run them through an interview process, where you let them know how long your manuscript is and what services you will need them to perform. Give them a short sample of five or ten pages, ask them to edit it and give you a quote for the whole project (including how long they think it will take them to complete the editing). When they give you back a product, choose the one that fits your time and budget constraints, while doing the best job editing your prose.

What should you pay? That depends on a lot of factors like the editor's experience and education level, and any specialized training they have, as well as what you want them to do. The Editorial Freelancers Association (EFA) publishes a rate card that shows an average range of fees for specific editing jobs, as well as for services like formatting, layout and fact checking. Part of their rate card (http://www.the-efa.org/res/rates.php) is included as Table 2.

Common Editing Rates		
Proofreading	9–13 pages/hour	$30–35/hour
Editing, basic copyediting	5–10 pages/hour	$30–40/hour
Editing, heavy copyediting	2–5 pages/hour	$40–50/hour
Editing, developmental	1–5 pages/hour	$45–55/hour

Table 2. Excerpt of EFA's 1/10/15 Rate Card

Based on the given rates, basic copyediting for a 300 page novel should take about 40 hours (at 7.5 pages/hour) and cost about $1,400 (at $35/hour). A more thorough developmental edit would average about $6,000 (2.5 pages/hour and $50/hour).

Although the rates are not extreme, based on experience and the value given by the editor, they are more than many beginning authors will be able to afford. Just because you can't afford the listed rates doesn't mean that every editor's rates are out of your range; a less experienced or less specialized editor might take on your project for less.

If you can afford it, a professional editor is the ideal way to go, and the one that I strongly recommend, especially if the book you are working on is your first. That is what I did, and I learned a number of things that helped me mature and improve as a writer. Although it is truly worth the money, often the price for a copy editor's most basic services will exceed a beginning author's fragile budget. What do you do then?

There are a variety of no-cost and low-cost options you can use to turn some of your time and talent into edits for your book. First, find a critique partner/circle or a writing group. There are a number of local- and national-level writing and critique groups you can join. As a writing circle/critique group member, you can have other members edit your book if you do the same for them.

Another way to get your book in front of other eyes is to enlist a group of beta readers. Try to develop a group that has skills in reading for content and character development, as well as spelling and grammar. Some people recommend using people who read the genre you're writing (who will be easier to find, as they like to read it); however, I would also suggest a reader or two that does *not* like your genre, especially if you are "hiring" readers that aren't professionals. Since they don't like your genre, they are less likely to get lost in the story and will remain true to their editing duties. I would shoot for four or five readers. Any less and your non-professionals are likely to miss things that need correction; if you use more, you may be faced with so many conflicting opinions that you have a hard time deciding what is right. If two of your beta readers agree, the issue is something you probably need to address.

While these two avenues give you additional sets of eyes on your book, it's important for me to re-emphasize that if you have any doubts about your writing, you should hire an editor. Yes, an editor is expensive (trust me, I know), but having your book edited is an investment in your writing career. Even if your first book doesn't pay off the bill, you are able to deduct the cost as a business expense, and your books will better represent you in the future. It's crucial to get your editing done right; you are not just affecting this one book's income stream, but the income streams of the rest of your books that follow.

Chapter 22 – You Can Do Better Than These 10 "Bad" "Things"

Your story is finished and you like it, generally, but for some reason your book lacks excitement in spots. Perhaps some of the words you use to describe characters or locations are lame. Whenever one of my editors sees the following words, he always says, "C'mon Chris, you can do better than that." As you go back through your masterpiece, do what you can to eliminate the following words:

Good/Bad. One of the most overused words in the English language is "good," because it is so good at describing a variety of subjects (see what I just did there?) Although it's easy to describe everything, over usage is what makes the word so vague. Some other substitutes are "worthy," "exceptional" or "excellent." The word "bad" is similarly...um, bad. Try words like "awful," "terrible" or "appalling" if they make sense.

New/Old. These two words are similar to good/bad, in that they are both very bland. Your writing will be more effective if you get rid of "new" and substitute words like "innovative" or "recent" instead. There are other words besides "old" that do a better job showing exactly how much time has gone by. If something is really aged, perhaps "ancient," "hoary" or "decrepit" might be more suitable.

Small/Big/Large. You can do better than "small." Try "miniature" or "tiny," or maybe even "microscopic" instead. Just like "old," being more specific could help out with "big" and "large." What about if the house was "immense," or maybe "massive?" Perhaps it might even be "enormous?"

Different. "Different" is another adjective that can be improved with more specificity. Is the object "rare" and "uncommon," or is it "bizarre" and "unusual?"

Things. "Things" also benefits from more specificity. Maybe the subjects are "objects" or perhaps they are someone's "belongings" or "property."

Seems. As will be seen in Chapter 24, not only is the word "seems" overused, it is also a filter word that takes the reader out of the story. Try a different word like "appears" or "shows signs of." Maybe the subject even "comes across as" something else.

Everyone is guilty of overusing these worn out words at some point; putting a little more variety into your writing will add spice. Similarly, people have their own "favorite" words they overuse; when you find yourself saying "awesome" for the 15th time, try something else.

Chapter 23 – Tightening Up Your Writing

Just as substituting more specific words for overused words will make your writing more exciting, getting rid of unnecessary words and redundancies will help tremendously with pacing and flow and will help your readers better understand a passage's meaning. There are a number of words and phrases we use that don't add meaning and/or hamper the flow of ideas; you should delete them when you find them.

First, don't build up your word count by using extra words when one word will do. "Although" is preferable to "in spite of the fact that" and "near" is better than "in the vicinity of." For example, "He parked the car in the vicinity of the old building, in spite of the fact that he knew it might fall down at some point in the near future," becomes "He parked the car near the old building although he knew it could collapse soon."

Next, skip the extra details that distract readers, leaving them wondering why the description is there, and whether the individual details are significant. The sentence, "A grimace appeared on his face as the soldier indicated with a gesture of his gun a truck that was to the left and behind the refugee," is incredibly long and confusing. Worse, most of it just isn't needed. The passage would be much better as "Grimacing, the soldier gestured to a truck behind the refugee."

Third, take out empty, "filler" words like "it was," "there were" and "that" whenever they're not needed. For example, "There was a closed door that stood at the end of the hall," becomes "A closed door stood at the end of the hall." The second sentence is much simpler, direct and active.

Fourth, delete any words or phrases that are redundant or unnecessarily reinforce what's already been said. "The truck was large *in size* and green *in color*, and it stood in the middle of the deserted street *with no one around*," can easily be condensed into "The large, green truck stood in the middle of the deserted street." This is far more concise *and to the point*.

Fifth, don't "tell" the readers something you've already shown them. For example, take the two sentences, "The little girl sat sulking on the couch, tears brimming in her eyes. She felt sad." The second sentence is redundant as it just restates (in a telling way) what the audience has already been shown.

Finally, condense any long-winded speeches. Normally, people don't speak in uninterrupted monologues (unless it's a parent yelling at a child). Try reading your dialogue out loud to ensure it sounds natural. If the conversation sounds like someone is quoting a Shakespearean soliloquy, the passage needs to be broken up. Think about how your character would speak in real life and make your prose match.

Chapter 24 – The Final Checks

As was already noted, the human mind is funny; when we proofread and edit our own writing, we tend to read our work as we *think* we wrote it, rather than the way we actually *did*. Because of this, we often don't see our spelling, grammar and punctuation mistakes, nor do we see the issues with word choice, sentence structure, context, and overall readability. Although the best way to ensure a good edit is to hire a professional proofreader or editor, sometimes that's not possible due to issues of money or time. If you are someone who puts out a lot of material (like a blogger or copywriter), proofreading and editing services can get expensive, and friends and family probably don't want to spend all their evenings checking your work. When you get to this point, you need a final checklist of your own to ensure you've done all you can to produce a quality product.

This chapter is going to cover a number of areas that will strengthen your writing. You cannot hope to catch everything in this chapter in a single pass, and it's unlikely you will spot them all in three or even five passes. That isn't the intent of this chapter. The guides and tips in this chapter are included to jog your memory. The odds are, you will probably publish your first book without addressing many of these issues (I did). Try to fix as many as you can, which will make your book stronger, and revisit this chapter periodically to better incorporate them into your writing style. They will serve you well over the long run, and your editors will thank you for the effort. To start with, here are seven quick tips for editing your own work:

1. Before you do any proofreading or editing, run your automatic spelling and grammar checker. Then, run the checker again after you're done to look for any mistakes you caused during your editing. You can't count on software to catch every spelling and grammar mistake, but it's a start.

2. Read your work aloud. Pronounce each word slowly and clearly and check for mistakes. If time allows, read the document backward, so you can see each word separately and out of context. If you don't have time, change the font to the boldest, ugliest font you have. This makes the prose harder to read and will help you concentrate on the words.

3. Never try to rush your proofreading and don't do it when you're tired or distracted. Only proofread when you're wide awake and have the time to do it correctly. Take periodic breaks to help you stay fresh.

4. Don't just review your book once and send it out. Your book should be edited until it reads smoothly,

with no errors; this level of excellence will probably require at least three read throughs.

5. Don't make any assumptions and don't be lazy. If you're not sure about spelling or grammar issues, look them up.

6. Don't forget to proofread titles, headlines and footnotes and make sure they match. This includes any headers at the top of your pages. Make sure your formatting is consistent throughout.

7. Take out passive voice anywhere you can. Active voice keeps a reader more engaged.

Once you've addressed these issues, do a fact check, regardless of whether your book is fiction or nonfiction. This should be a front-to-back fact check that ensures what you said is the same as what you meant, which is the same as reality. Most nonfiction books are full of information, making this check mandatory, but fiction writers also need to check their facts. For example, I write military books which feature people with ranks. Are these consistent throughout? If someone gets killed or wounded in Book One of a series, do they resurface hale and hearty in the second book? Those are both errors of fact (and fairly embarrassing, as well).

Next, fix any word choice problems that still exist. You can either do this with a read through, or use your word processing software to find instances of the words you know are problems for you. Some words to watch out for are:

Almost–Avoid having people "almost" doing things; have them actively do them, instead.

Among/Between–Use "among" when you have more than two things/people. Use "between" when there are exactly two.

Began to/Started to–Unless the intent is to interrupt them in the process, characters should do things, not start to do them.

Causing–Avoid writing "Something happened, causing a second action to happen." The word "causing" takes the reader out of the action.

Compared with/to–When you are pointing out differences, use "compared with." For similarities, use "compared to."

Due to–Usually, "because of" is correct.

Each and every–Do not use outside of dialogue, as it adds extra words with little meaning.

Inside of–Don't use "of" if you're talking about location. The phrase "inside of" means "in less than." For example, the soldier is "inside" the tent preparing; the attack should commence "inside of" one hour.

Nearly–Once again, your characters should do things, not almost do them.

Nor–Nor should follow an instance of "neither."

Not–Write actively and affirmatively; avoid "not" where possible (for example, "He stayed home," rather than "He did not go.")

Not only...but also–"Not only" is a correlative conjunction that requires the use of "but also," as well as two verbs that make chronological sense, two adjectives, or two nouns. Both clauses have to be parallel.

Once more/Again/Once again–Only use if they add something to or clarify the meaning of the story.

One of the most/The fact that–Both should usually be deleted.

That/Which–"That" is used to set off a restrictive clause, while "which" sets off a non-restrictive clause. If the clause isn't needed for meaning or clarification (non-restrictive), then "which" is used. If the first part of the sentence requires clarification, or the subsequent clause provides important information, it is a restrictive clause and the word "that" is used.

Whether or not/Whether–In most cases, the "or not" isn't needed.

The next check is to eliminate unnecessary qualifiers. You will find them with weak adjectives or nouns, often indicating something stronger should be used. Consider finding a stronger word if you find any of the following qualifiers:

a bit	more
(a good/great) deal	most
enough	pretty
even	quite
fairly	rather
indeed	really
just	so
kind of/sort of	somewhat
least	still
less	too
(a) little	very
a (whole) lot	

The next task is to remove filter words. What's a filter word? It's a word that unnecessarily filters the reader's experience through a character's point of view. Filtering is when you place a character between the detail you want to present and the reader. Here's a list of filter words:

To See (See, Sees, Saw, Seeing, Seen)
To Hear (Hear, Hears, Heard, Hearing)
To Feel (Feel, Feels, Felt, Feeling)
To Look (Look, Looks, Looked, Looking)
To Know (Know, Knows, Knew, Knowing)
To Think (Think, Thinks, Thought, Thinking)
To Wonder (Wonder, Wonders, Wondered, Wondering)
To Realize (Realize, Realizes, Realized, Realizing)
To Watch (Watch, Watches, Watched, Watching)
To Notice (Notice, Notices, Noticed, Noticing)
To Seem (Seem, Seems, Seemed, Seeming)
To Decide (Decide, Decides, Decided, Deciding)
To Sound (Sound, Sounds, Sounded, Sounding)

For example, "Sarah **felt** a sinking feeling in her stomach as she **realized** she'd forgotten her purse back at the house." Eliminating the filter words leaves you with, "Sarah's stomach sank. Her purse—she'd forgotten it back at the house." As you can see, eliminating the filter words removes the filters that distance readers from the character's experience, greatly improving the writing. Admittedly, there are going to be exceptions to this rule, and even though filter words are weak they may still be useful at times...but it is usually better to find a stronger verb to replace them with when you can.

A final weak construction to avoid is the "Something of Something." If you see prose like "the handle of the door" or the "ears of the cat," you can (and should) simplify them, often by using the possessive. The two preceding examples become the "door handle" and the "cat's ears." Both are simpler and read easier.

Wow! This chapter covered an enormous amount of information; so much, in fact, you are probably wondering how you will ever remember it all! As I indicated at the beginning of the chapter, at first you probably won't, and that is okay. As you find yourself mastering some of these tips, you are encouraged to return and find new issues to address.

Covering Your Gem

"You can't judge a book by its cover." Although everyone's heard this saying, nothing could be further from the truth. Everyone judges books by their covers. In fact, it has been estimated more than half of your sales are due to your cover alone; you need to have a great cover if you want your book to be successful. Your book is competing with every other book that's been published, including those backed by major publishing houses with massive budgets. Nothing could be more important than a good cover since it's the first thing a reader sees when he or she goes shopping. You could have the best blurb in the world, but if your cover isn't captivating enough to get readers to pick up your book, they will never see it. If your cover isn't any good, your sales won't be, either. Paying for a professional cover designer is well worth your money, as it's crucial to have an excellent cover that hits your target market. People *do* judge books by their covers; you need one that is going to sell books.

Chapter 25 – Book Covers and Knowing What Sells

Before we talk about the cover, let's start with the title (assuming you don't already have one). You want something catchy, yet different. While you *can* use a title that's been used before, you probably don't want to, as readers will have to weed through the ones that are already out there to find yours. Additionally, shorter titles are generally better than longer ones; longer titles can work, but they need to be easy to remember.

If you're writing a series, it's a good idea to develop a title you can expand or play off when you're developing future titles. I didn't do that with my *Theogony* science fiction trilogy, but that was because my designer and I had already figured out the cover art—it was one picture cut into thirds so that the three books form a planet-scape if they are placed on a table next to each other.

Can't decide on a title? This is where your early readers, blog readers or fans can help. If you get stumped, develop two or three options and put them out for a public vote. Usually, there will be a majority for one of the titles; that one is your best choice for a marketable title. Once you've settled on a title, you've also gone a long way toward determining your cover art.

Before you work any further on designing the cover, you need to know what other covers in your genre look like. Your cover is an indication of your genre and should fit within the genre in terms of what is portrayed, how it is depicted and what fonts are used. If you walk through a book store, you will have a pretty good idea of which section you're in just by looking at the covers. Even though science fiction and fantasy themes are somewhat similar and sometimes cross over, the covers are vastly different. Neither of these, however, would be confused with a romance novel or a cookbook. Each genre has its own special "look." Before you decide on how you want your cover to appear, go to a book store or look on Amazon and browse the covers in your genre. See what works and what doesn't. If a cover makes you want to pick up a book, it will probably make other people want to pick up the book, as well.

Here are a few other items to keep in mind as you put together your cover. First, it *has* to look professional, or no one is going to buy your book. If your cover looks second rate, your book sales *will* be affected. Most people focus on the visual, and they will gravitate toward the picture and not the title. If they can't see the image clearly in the tiny Amazon thumbnail, potential buyers are going to skip right over it. What are buyers looking for? There are five key elements winning book covers have. They must capture the reader's attention, evoke emotions, hint at the story, be visually pleasing and be simple (while still accomplishing all of the preceding imperatives).

First, the cover has to capture the reader's attention. If it doesn't look professional, readers probably aren't going to look any further at the book. Even if they do, the fact you have a sub-par cover will be on their minds as they read the blurb and/or sample. The image displayed should be representative of the genre's target market. Is it similar to the top selling titles in your genre? For example, if you were writing a romance novel, you would want an image of love, romance and a hunk that grabs your female readers. Got a horror book? You need a dark, sinister, threatening cover geared more toward males.

Second, your cover should evoke emotions and make readers feel something. There's a reason romance books have hunks on their covers; it's to arouse feelings. This is the same reason horror books have clowns with bloody knives (although the images generate *very* different feelings). Both covers appeal to potential readers' emotions, drawing them in to see what the book's all about.

Third, a good cover hints at the story. Readers will only look at your book cover for a couple of seconds before either selecting it or moving on, and they are usually only looking at a thumbnail-sized version. In that time, your cover has to set the mood of the book and give readers a little of the story. Depending on the genre, the mood is sometimes enough. An empty rowboat vanishing into a thick fog would set the mood for a mystery/suspense book and could be a great cover, as long as it matches the story.

Fourth, in addition to the three elements above, the cover has to be visually pleasing. There are many books that have attractive cover images, but lose the reader with text colors that clash or don't work with the background. Perhaps their authors think the covers will be "memorable" or "unique" and will get readers to purchase the books because of their uniqueness, but in most cases those covers just come across as tacky or loud, and readers skip over them.

Finally, it's best if your cover is simple and features a single scene or image that captures the theme of the book. If your cover is too cluttered, readers won't be able to tell what's going on in the thumbnail. One strong image is usually much better than several images competing for space, making the design confusing and cluttered. If you can't read the title or author's name through all of the clutter, you're probably doing it wrong.

One additional note on cover design. If you're planning a series, you need to consider where you are going with the series before you choose the final design for the first book, as you will probably want to coordinate the covers. Any stock art to be purchased for subsequent covers should be acquired now to ensure it will be available when needed. If you buy a pre-made cover, make sure the overall setup isn't hard to replicate for the structure of subsequent books.

Got an idea for your front cover? We'll take a look at creating it in the next two chapters. The blurb for the back cover will be covered in Unit 7.

Chapter 26 – Commissioning Your Cover: Elance

So now you know what you want on your cover, and you're ready to make it happen. There are a host of graphic designers and specialty cover designers you can use to design a great cover, most of whom will provide great value for your money. If you decide to use one of these, check out their previous work and see how it compares with the industry standard. Get a reference or two to see how they were to work with and their policies on changes.

If you choose not to use a graphic designer, another option is to use one of the freelancer websites like Elance or 99Designs. This chapter will look at Elance (www.elance.com), which is a web-based service that connects freelancers with hiring managers. All an author has to do is create an account and post a job offering and bam! You're a hiring manager. You set the time frame for how long you'll accept proposals and then the bidding begins. The site allows you to set a price range, or you can let the bidding fluctuate without bounds. In many cases, the offers at the top of the bidding range are qualitatively no different than the proposals at the bottom. The most important detail of the process is to make sure the terms of service state that once you approve the work and pay the artist, all of the intellectual property rights are transferred to the hiring manager (you). That is, you own and can do whatever you want with the cover once you pay for it.

How do you audition the talent? It's pretty easy on Elance. When designers submit their proposals, they also include links to their portfolios on Elance and external sites. You should review their portfolios and find an artist who has a style that speaks to you. If an artist's covers don't conjure any emotions in you, they probably won't do so for your audience, either. Unless you feel you can mentor someone new to cover design through the process, it's important to make sure the artist you're considering has experience creating book covers. If you don't have the knowledge, experience or time to guide someone through the process, you'll be much better off hiring a seasoned artist.

Even though you're the author and not the cover designer, you still need to have an idea of what you want to see on your cover, and how the design should be portrayed. Your artist isn't a mind reader, and you need to be prepared with a thorough design brief. The brief will answer basic questions and give the designer general guidance on what you're looking for. It should have all the information needed to complete your cover: the title, the back cover copy, the scene description, any emotions to be conveyed, any technical or visual specifications ("at least 300 dots per inch," "title must be legible as a thumbnail") and the entire Elance job description. It's important to be as specific as possible with your job description, as you don't want to have to renegotiate things later. If both parties know exactly what is expected and required from the start, things will go much more smoothly. If you don't know what to include, look at previous design packages until you find an ultra-detailed template you can use. It's better to include too much information than not enough.

Above all else, make sure you're happy with the cover before you give final approval. If *you* don't like the cover, your readers probably won't, either!

Chapter 27 – Commissioning Your Cover: 99Designs

Another site you can use for cover design is 99Designs, which I used for my last two covers. I am a fan, as the design process results in excellent covers at a great price. With 99Designs, you develop your cover by means of a contest, in which designers compete to create the winning submission.

After building a personal profile, the author puts together a design brief. Most of the information is straightforward, with the exception of the "Notes" section. This is the place where it pays to be as detailed as possible. Start out with what you want designed. Give the artists a concept but leave them enough room to use their creativity. After that, make sure you put in the technical specifications. When I get a cover designed, I want to get an ebook cover, a print cover and an audio book cover done at the same time, so I ask for all three types as part of my package. Usually, I am only putting out the print and ebook copies in the beginning, but if I intend to do an audio book, I include the requirement for an audio cover in the design brief so I have the cover when I need it. Here's what the technical part of the "Notes" section for my last book looked like:

Technical information. Three files are required. One for the ebook, one for the print book and one for the audio book.

1. eBook Cover (for Amazon Kindle):
a. Media: JPEG.
b. Resolution: 2820x4500 pixels.
2. Audio book:
a. Media: JPEG.
b. Resolution: 2400x2400 pixels.
3. 5.5" x 8.5" Print Book:
a. Media: JPEG.

b. Resolution: 1600x2400 pixels, with a minimum resolution of 300 DPI.

c. Safe Zone. Text and images must be at least .125" inside the trim lines to ensure that no live elements are cut during the bookmaking process.

Unlike ebooks that only have the front cover, print books have a back cover as well as a spine. When you commission your cover, you need to decide whether to have just the front cover designed or the whole wraparound book cover (which includes the front, spine and back cover). If making the wraparound cover, you should make sure the designer leaves room on the back for where the ISBN bar code goes.

Which one should you choose? I would have the entire cover made so that all of the pieces work well together. If you only have the front cover designed (like the example above), you have to worry about matching it to one of CreateSpace's stock designs, which is sometimes difficult. The only drawback to designing a wraparound print cover is that you must know all of your book's information (like the number of pages and whether you're going to use white or cream paper) when you commission the cover in order for the designer to size it correctly. Because of this, cover design can only occur late in the book preparation process.

The "Notes" section should also include the competition criteria. Stating these up front makes the process fair for all. One last item to add to the "Notes" section is whether you are guaranteeing the prize. With 99Designs, you can choose to wait and see what the covers look like before deciding if there will be a winner, or you can guarantee there will be a winner (and a payout). While guaranteeing the prize requires you to take it on faith that one cover will be good enough to win, if you don't offer this guarantee, you will have a harder time getting the better designers to participate. I always guarantee the prize and haven't had a hard time getting designers. For the last competition, I had ten designers participate and received 29 designs.

After filling out the design brief, you select a design package. You have four levels to choose from: bronze, silver, gold and platinum. Each succeeding level costs more, but is supposed to give you access to higher quality designers because a higher price results in a bigger paycheck for the designer. I have only used the bronze level ($299); however, I have been very happy with the cover proposals I received. Of note, $99 is kept by the site (regardless of the level), and the remainder of the fee is the prize the winning designer receives.

When you launch your contest, 99Designs posts your information on their marketplace where "more than 888,000 creative professionals from Berlin to Bombay will read your brief and begin to brainstorm ideas just for you." The first part of the competition, which lasts four days, is on. Artists will now begin to submit their ideas for your cover. As the artists are located worldwide, designs will arrive around the clock. You will need to periodically log into your account to see what's been submitted. What can you do to increase the number of submissions? Go through 99Designs' list of book cover designers, search for those who have created covers you like and invite them to your contest. If you've guaranteed the prize, let them know; they will be more likely to participate. There's a limit to how many you can invite, but you should invite as many as you can every day for the first couple of days to maximize your contest's participation. It doesn't hurt to stroke their egos—tell them how impressed you are with their work, and that they'd be perfect for your project.

As the designs begin to come in, make sure you're rating all of them and providing feedback on what you like and don't like. You can use the star ratings, comments and private messages to help designers shape their ideas to your needs. The more detailed your feedback, the better the artists will be able to bring your cover to life; good feedback will also help guide the ones that haven't submitted yet. This process goes on for four days, and then you have to choose which designers to take to the final round. You can take up to six, but I've never had more than four that were still "in it" at that point.

The second round only lasts three days, giving the designers you selected a little more time to work with you and design a cover you like. The second round is like the first, but with fewer competitors remaining so you can focus on the best designs.

At the end of the second round the contest ends, and you pick the winner. The two of you sign the copyright agreement, the designer transfers the file to you and 99Designs transfers the prize money to the designer. You can then download your new design and use it in whatever ways you'd like.

Publishing Your Ebook

Your story is done and your cover is ready. It's almost time to turn on that big revenue tap, and let your readers shower you with their gratitude for creating such a masterpiece. Even if the royalties don't initially flow in with the force of a hydrant, at least it will be satisfying to finally get your book "out there." There are just a few more considerations before you do so.

Chapter 28 – ISBN and the ASIN

As you get ready to publish, one of the things you need to decide is whether to purchase an ISBN for your book. What's an ISBN? As mentioned previously, a book's International Standard Book Number (ISBN) is nothing more than a way of tracking and identifying it. ISBNs are 13 digit numbers (10 digits before January, 2007) that identify items like the book's publisher and country of origin. What each digit means is beyond the scope of this book; what's important is you know an ISBN is a unique 13-digit number used to identify a specific edition of a book by booksellers, libraries and distributors around the world.

In the United States, the R.R. Bowker Company issues ISBNs, which are purchased during the publishing process and assigned to a book. Yes, I did say "purchased;" there is a cost that varies depending upon the number of ISBNs you buy. A single ISBN costs $125, while 10 ISBNs cost $275, 100 ISBNs cost $575 and 1,000 ISBNs cost $1,000. No one knows why the price per unit drops from $125 for one to only $1 if you buy 1,000, although many have asked. A conspiracy theorist would say it is probably to help keep independent publishers out of the market; who else would want to buy one or two ISBNs at a time? Publishing houses buy them in large quantities, so the system would certainly seem to be rigged in their favor. And why the relatively high cost? It's not like there are a lot of materials or labor that go into making an ISBN; you are only purchasing the use of a number.

So, $125 for an ISBN. I'm sure you're asking yourself, "Do I really need one of these?' While you don't *need* to have one to publish a book, you *want* to have an ISBN for your book, and you are probably going to need more than one. Why? Two reasons. The first is that if you plan to sell your book to bookstores or libraries, or if you'll be selling through online retailers like Amazon.com (and you will), the retailers will require an ISBN to identify your book. The second reason is having an ISBN gives your book (and you) credibility. In self-publishing, credibility is vitally important to selling your book; an ISBN is one of the ways you get it.

Why will you need more than one ISBN? Not only are you going to be writing lots of books (Chapter 40), but you are also going to need one for each of the book's formats. Got an ebook version? That's one. Print copy? That's two. Going to turn your book into an audio book? Yes, you are, so that's three. As you can see, you're probably going to be buying at least ten of them, knocking the price down to $27.50 each (which still isn't a bargain for something that is nothing more than a number, but at least it's better than $125 per ISBN).

So, how do you get an ISBN? It's easy. You go to https://www.myidentifiers.com, which is Bowker's ISBN website. Click on "ISBN" in the top menu, and you'll be given the choice of whether to buy 1, 10, 100 or 1,000 (or more!) ISBNs. You are also given the choice of getting them made into bar codes for your books (for an additional fee, of course). You don't need this option as bar codes will be created for you in the publishing process (for free!)

When you are ready to publish your book, you will return to the Bowker site and register your title. When you do this, the information about your book is stored in Bowker's Books in Print database, which makes it available to retailers, libraries, Bowker Books in Print, Bookwire and to online services like Google Books, Apple's iBooks and the New York Times.

I'm sure you have a lot of questions about ISBNs; I will try to address the common ones. First, is having an ISBN the same as having a copyright on the work? No, these are different. An ISBN is an identifier for your book that is used by people in the literary industry to distinguish the individual edition of it. A copyright, on the other hand, is the exclusive legal entitlement an author has to an original work's use and distribution for a period of time, which ensures the author is compensated for the intellectual effort. So, what do you need to do to get a copyright on your novel? Register? Pay a lot of money? No, all you need to do is "nothing." The Berne Convention, of which the U.S. is a party, says an author does not need to register or apply for a copyright; instead, once the work is "fixed," (i.e., written or recorded in a physical medium), the author is automatically entitled to all copyrights for the book and any derivatives.

Another question beginning authors often have is whether an ISBN can be reused once a book has gone out of print, or you no longer want to sell it. Unfortunately, the answer is "no." Once an ISBN has been assigned, the ISBN can never be reused. But what if you revise your book? Does the book need a new ISBN? The answer is "maybe," depending on the number and scope of changes in the revision. If you don't make any substantial changes to the text (say the revision was only to fix some typographical errors), then you don't need a new ISBN because the book is considered a reprint. Substantially changing the document's text, like adding or removing chapters, creates a new edition, and the resulting "new" book would require a new ISBN. It is interesting to note that changing the cover does *not* result in a new edition; since the text has not changed, you can continue to use the same ISBN.

But what if you use the ISBN for a digital version of the book and then you decide you want to publish a print copy. Can you use the same for both? Once again, the answer is "no." At least for now, you need a separate ISBN for each format the book is in (hard cover, soft cover, digital and audio) to identify it from the others.

So that's an ISBN. What's the difference between an ISBN and the other identifier you see on Amazon, a book's ASIN? While the ISBN is an industry standard method of identifying the edition of a book, the Amazon Standard Identification Number (ASIN) is a 10-character alphanumeric identifier assigned by Amazon.com and its partners for product identification within the Amazon.com organization.

ASINs are used in Amazon's various storefronts, like Amazon.uk (for the United Kingdom) and Amazon.ca (for Canada). Although ASINs used to be unique worldwide, global expansion has changed the standard to where an ASIN is only guaranteed to be unique within an individual marketplace. The same book may be referred to by several ASINs as different national sites may use different ASINs for the same product.

Within Amazon.com, each product is given a unique ASIN. For print books with 10-digit ISBNs, the ASIN and the ISBN are the same. This is different than the Kindle edition of a book, which will not use its ISBN as its ASIN.

Chapter 29 – The Blurb

Don't know what a blurb is? It's the description on the back of your book, and it's an important element of your marketing package. It's what hooks readers in, so having an enticing book description is a necessary part of your sales process. An enticing blurb has four elements:

1. **Situation**. The first part of your blurb is a simple description of what's going on, showing potential readers where the story occurs, and who the main characters are.

2. **Problem**. The next piece of the blurb identifies a challenge or difficulty that makes the situation untenable or brings about conflict. This part usually starts with "But…" or "However…" or "Until…"

3. **The slimmest chance**. This element is the hook that makes your audience want to know more. Even though the situation (#1) seems doomed by the problem (#2), there is still hope that things will turn out all right because of this unlikely event or this person's weird ability. Together, these first three elements create the drama that propels the story.

4. **Mood or tone**. This element lets readers know what emotional state they're going to be in while reading the book. Is it a dark and foreboding tale of horror, or is it a tense but entertaining thriller? The blurb converts book browsers into book buyers.

That's all there is to it. If you follow this template, you will be well on your way to designing a great blurb. As an example, here's the blurb I designed for my novel, *Janissaries:*

(#1) The war with China was over, and Lieutenant Shawn 'Calvin' Hobbs just wanted his life to go back to normal. The hero of the war, he had a small ream of paperwork to fill out, a deployment with his Navy F-18 squadron to prepare for, and a new girlfriend to spend some quality time with. Life was good. (#2) Until the aliens showed up. (#3) They had a ship and needed to get to their home planet, but didn't have a crew. They had seen Calvin's unit in action during the war, though, and knew it was the right one for the job. There was just one small problem—a second race of aliens was coming, which would end all life on Earth. Calvin's platoon might want to do something about that, too. Having won a terrestrial war with 30 troops, winning an interstellar war with nothing but a 3,000 year old cruiser should be easy, right? (#4) *Janissaries* initiates *The Theogony*, a trilogy that takes Lieutenant Hobbs and his Special Forces platoon to the stars where they will learn that there's much more to Earth's history than is written in the history books!

As you can see, it's not hard to put a blurb together if you know how. There are two last points to keep in mind. First, keep your description short. The *Janissaries* blurb is actually a little on the long side, something self-published authors tend to do. Don't overload the reader with too much information; less is more. Second, the best blurbs are dramatic. Readers want to have drama; they want to feel the tension. They want to be enticed with the appetizer of the blurb so they know the main course of the novel will keep them hooked until the end. If your blurb doesn't grab them, readers will assume your book won't either.

Your blurb should receive the same treatment as the rest of the novel, especially since readers will use it to make their purchase decisions. No matter how good you are at blurb-writing, therefore, you need to have your blurb edited. Once it's ready, test your blurb out on your fans to get their reactions. Does it grab them? If so, you have a winner!

What if your book is nonfiction? What are the elements of a nonfiction blurb? A nonfiction blurb is slightly different, as it will tell readers what problem the book will solve, as well as why the readers have the problem, common obstacles to solving the problem and how the book will help readers overcome their obstacles. The blurb should also list some other benefits readers will receive from reading the book, tell them something else about the problem they didn't already know and establish why you're the best person to help them. It should also include examples that support the above elements.

One last note. If you are writing a blurb for a non-lead book of a series, don't assume that the reader is familiar with the books that preceded it. Just like a non-lead book has to have enough information at the start to bring new readers up to speed with the series, the blurb must do so, too. Make sure both the book and the book description for each book in a series can stand on their own.

Chapter 30 – What Price, Perfection?

One of the many things authors agonize over is what price they should set for their book. Should you go with something high and try to get everything you can, or should you price your book at 99 cents and go for maximum distribution? Should you do something in between? Personally, I've worked too hard to give my books away on Amazon for 99 cents. At that price point, you only get 35% of the royalties generated by the book's sales, rather than the 70% you receive when the price is $2.99 or higher. To me, my time is worth more than 35 cents. I submit that if you price your book for less than $2.99, you are cheating yourself (and the other authors holding the line). You also take away your ability to run a sale. If you only charge 99 cents to start with, you don't have much leeway to drop the price for a sales promotion.

Overpricing your book is similarly dangerous. Unless you have a name like "Stephen King," pricing your book at $9.99 or above probably won't work. While you may be tempted to set your price high, one of the goals of your first book is to develop a following. You want to attract as many people as possible to read your book, review it and talk about it with their friends. When your next book comes out, you want them to be there to buy it and read it, as well. If they've never heard of you and your book is priced too high, they are unlikely to buy it, regardless of how good your marketing is.

An internet search on the topic reveals much discussion on what should be charged, but little agreement. Most people seem to place the price somewhere between $2.99 and $3.99 for genre fiction books (with nonfiction books being slightly higher). This allows authors to get the most profit for their books, while still giving good value to readers. If your book doesn't sell in this range, it doesn't mean it's over-priced. More likely, your marketing efforts weren't very good or very timely, or your cover or blurb (or both) wasn't good enough. Do *not* drop your price out of fear that you set it too high. Instead, refocus your marketing efforts and rework your cover or blurb if you see they are the reason your book is not selling. Do not drop your prices. That doesn't mean you can't run specials for a short time or use other marketing tools, but only use these discounted prices for a defined time before resetting your price to what it was.

What's the best thing you can do if your book isn't selling? Write another book, as we will discuss in Chapter 40.

Chapter 31 – Publishing your Ebook

I'd like to tell you formatting your book for uploading onto the ebook retailer sites is a simple, easy process. I can't, but while I can't tell you it's simple, it's not *that* difficult either, especially if you used the format guide recommended in Unit 4 (in which case, you're all set for Amazon!). Before we discuss formatting, let's take a second and talk about retailers. Which sites do you want to use?

Amazon is a no-brainer, as the giant controls almost 2/3 of the ebook market. More than 95% of the ebooks I've sold have been through Amazon. Not only will it sell your books in the United States, Amazon will also market your books for free in 12 foreign countries. You need to have your book there. The choice you have to make is whether you want to be single source with Amazon and enroll your book in the Kindle Direct Publishing Select program (KDP Select) or if you want to distribute your book as widely as possible.

By choosing KDP Select, you are agreeing to make your book exclusive to the Kindle Store for at least 90 days. If you do so, the book is eligible to be included in the Kindle

Owners' Lending Library, and you will earn a share of Amazon's monthly fund, based on how frequently the book is borrowed. You won't get paid as much as you would have for a full price sale, but your book becomes more accessible to readers in the program as they can access it for free. In addition, by choosing KDP Select, you will have the ability to use a variety of promotional tools, including offering enrolled books for free to readers for up to 5 days every 90 days.

KDP Select allows you to distribute your book on a no-risk basis to people who might not otherwise have tried it, but there is an opportunity cost as you aren't allowed to make the ebook available on any other site. People with Nook readers will never see your book, as it won't be on Barnes & Noble's website, nor will your book be available on any of the other ebook retailer sites. Is that a worthwhile tradeoff? Maybe. I've tried both ways and have had mixed success. It's hard to judge, as you cannot know how many sales you lost on the other sites by being exclusive with Amazon. For a first book, there is something to be said for trying KDP Select, as the service doesn't charge readers for trying your book, something they might not have done otherwise.

One additional note of caution is, with the launch of Kindle Unlimited, Amazon is changing some of the rules of the game. Many pundits believe that the pay per view will continue to drop, making KDP Select a much worse option. Many independent authors (including some of the big names) are leaving KDP Select, and only time will tell whether KDP Select will remain a viable option.

If you choose to look beyond Amazon, where else would you want to place your ebook? I like to upload my books onto Barnes & Noble and then use Smashwords to distribute to the rest of the digital retailers. Barnes & Noble is my second largest retailer, so it makes sense for me to upload my ebook to their site. And, while Smashwords takes a percentage of my sales, they upload my work to all of the small retailers, something I don't have the time or desire to do. I simply upload my ebook to the Smashwords website, and they distribute it to 11 other retailers like Apple, Kobo and Scribd.

Unfortunately, each of these retailers likes having books on their site formatted in slightly different ways. How do you know what they want? Each retailer has a free guide on its website. As mentioned in Unit 4, for Amazon's Kindle, the guide is "Building your book for Kindle." At the time this book went to press, the latest version was at: http://www.amazon.com/dp/B007URVZJ6. For Barnes & Noble, there is a pamphlet called "Formatting Guidelines for Microsoft Word Documents," which is located at https://www.nookpress.com/support. For Smashwords, you can look at "The Smashwords Style Guide," which can be found at https://www.smashwords.com/books/view/52. Each of these details how to format your ebook in Word so it converts correctly. They also show you how to put in the front matter (the stuff before the story, like the dedication) and the back matter (the things after the story). At the very least, you want to make sure that your back matter has a page with links to your website and the Amazon pages of any other books you have published.

Once you have your book in the proper format, the upload process is usually pretty easy. The only retailer I've had difficulty with is Smashwords, which uses "the Meatgrinder" to convert your book. Smashwords distributes to a large number of retailers so everything has to be perfect for your book to get through their process unscathed. It's possible to get it through the Meatgrinder on the first try if you have great attention to detail. Possible...but not likely. Don't worry if your story fails the first time. You're not in school, and no one is keeping score; just fix any identified issues and resubmit.

One last point prior to uploading your ebook is that the categories you pick for it will be key to how well your book performs on Amazon, and whether it gets picked up for the various lists and marketing tools that Amazon provides. You do NOT want to put your book in the broadest category. Doing so will not help it reach the widest audience; instead, the opposite is true. By picking a broad category, you will be compared with more books, driving your ranking so far down that you won't ever make it out of the noise at the bottom of the rankings. Instead, you want to be the big fish in the little pond; narrow your audience by choosing the smallest sub- or sub-sub-category that is relevant, so your book has a chance of making its mark.

With that in mind, it's time to upload your manuscript onto the sites you have chosen. If you want to upload your ebook onto any of the other sites beyond the ones I use (which I hope you do), please do. I hope you have good luck on them; I have heard anecdotal evidence that Apple's iTunes site is great for some genres (like Romance), but I haven't sold more than a handful of books there. Like everything else in self-publishing, your experience may be different, and you need to experiment to find out what works best for you.

Uploading your manuscript to Amazon is easy, and there are detailed instructions in the style guide to assist you if needed. Just go to https://kdp.amazon.com/ and sign in (if you don't have an account, you will need to create one). Once you have logged in, you will be brought to the "Bookshelf" screen. From there, click on "Add new title" and follow the steps. If you have all of your information (manuscript file, cover, blurb and ISBN), it only takes about 10 minutes to add all of the data. When you click on the "Save and Publish" button, congratulations! You are now a published author!

Take a moment to celebrate...then set up your Amazon site and get back to writing your next book.

Chapter 32 – Optimizing Amazon: Literary Life or Death

Known as 'The Algorithm,' Amazon's internal marketing system is without peer. Amazon's system uses sales (and some people say reviews and other inputs) to decide which books to promote and how much visibility to give to each (in listings, emails and so forth). Getting noticed by The Algorithm has a major effect on your book sales. How big a difference? It's hard to tell (since sales data are proprietary, as is anything to do with The Algorithm), but the difference is certainly in the thousands of sales. In fact, the sales increase is probably bigger than any other advertising campaign you could set up, so it is extremely important to do everything you can to get Amazon to promote you. One simple thing you can do to ensure your success is to fill out all of your Amazon Pages completely and correctly. You may not become an Amazon bestseller if you do them, but if you don't, your book won't be as successful as it could be.

The first of these pages is your Author Page (https://authorcentral.amazon.com/gp/home), which is where your readers are able to learn more about you and your books. The page lets you post a variety of information about your life, including a biography, photos, blog feeds, videos, twitter posts and event listings (for virtual and in-person events). The Author Page also has images and links to all of your titles on Amazon in all of the formats in which they are available. In addition to the ebook/Kindle format, you may have print books available (from CreateSpace or Spark) as well as audio books (available from Audible). It's almost as if Amazon were hosting a secondary website for you.

One of the biggest mistakes authors make is to substitute a picture of one of their books in the "Photo" slot instead of a picture of themselves. Even if you don't like the way you look, this is still a mistake. Readers want to connect with the author, and they are more likely to purchase a book if they see a picture of the author (regardless of what we look like, believe it or not). A head and shoulders shot is favored with an open and friendly expression. Make sure they can see your eyes!

Got a picture posted? Good, now work on your profile. In addition to telling people about yourself, the goal is to try to be compelling while still being true to yourself. After that, ensure any extras are loaded. Got any videos or book trailers? How about a twitter feed? All of this information helps a reader learn to trust you as a writer.

Lastly, the book descriptions or blurbs you post on this site are some of the most important pieces of writing you will do. These tiny bits of prose are central to your self-publishing efforts. Make sure you take the time to do them well!

Other Formats

Ebooks are wonderful, and at some point they may replace print books (the jury is still out on when, exactly). I love ebooks as they have been responsible for almost 95% of my sales. However, there are other formats in which you can sell your story, and if you don't go any further, you are going to short-change yourself out of a ton of revenue you could have had. This unit will discuss other formats besides the ebook. I wish I had known these were so easy back when I started!

Chapter 33 – Beyond the Digital World

You're a published author! Unfortunately, many authors get so focused on publishing their ebooks on Amazon they go no further. They don't recognize all the additional ways they can make money from the same manuscript.

One of the great things about a book is it's tremendously scalable. What's scalability? It's the ability to sell the same thing many times. Not only will you earn money from the sale of your digital book for the rest of your life (and well beyond, thanks to the copyright laws), you can also use your book to create a number of other income streams.

In all likelihood, the Amazon ebook is going to be your biggest source of royalty income, but that doesn't mean you have to stop there. Even if you selected the KDP Select when you published your story, after 90 days you can remove your ebook from the system and make it available on other platforms like Kobo, the iBookstore, Nook and Scribd. These retailers are easy to use, and the process to upload your book to their sites is usually pretty simple. If you need to convert your Word document to a different file type, you can create the new format yourself using tools like Scrivener or Calibre (I like Calibre and it is free and easy), or by paying for someone to convert your book for you.

As discussed earlier, if you would rather have a simpler approach than spending several hours uploading your book across all of these sites (most of which, admittedly, aren't going to sell a lot of copies), you can use a retailer like Smashwords (https://www.smashwords.com/) or BookBaby (http://www.bookbaby.com/), which will upload your ebook to all of the main retailers. This comes at a price, as Smashwords takes a 10% commission and BookBaby takes 15% to distribute your book, but that may be a small price to pay so that you can upload your book once and let their systems do all of the distribution leg work.

What do I do? As mentioned, I go direct with Amazon and Barnes & Noble, my two biggest retailers, and I use

Smashwords for all the rest, opting in to all of the available channels except for those two. I don't sell enough on the other systems for it to be worth my time to update them every time I put out a new release or edition to my books. Beyond Smashwords, you can also use Bookbaby's free option to distribute your books to the retailers Smashwords doesn't cover, like Copia, e-Sentral and Gardners Books.

But don't stop at just producing an ebook; there's that old standby that has existed for thousands of years—the printed book. Although its image may have tarnished recently, there are still many people (like me) who would rather hold a book in their hands while they enjoy it. A decade ago, publishing a print book meant a significant investment in both money and floor space, as the author was forced to pay for the print run of thousands of books in order to get print copies...and then provide warehousing in his or her home until the books sold. If they didn't sell, the author was left with boxes and boxes of unwanted books. Happily, this is no longer necessary.

Now, with the advent of print-on-demand technology, authors don't have to pay upfront for print runs or worry about having to store and ship physical products. Instead, when a book is ordered, one copy is printed and sent directly to the purchaser, and you, the author, receive your royalty. The two biggest companies that provide print-on-demand services are CreateSpace (https://www.createspace.com/) and Ingram Spark (https://www1.lightningsource.com/default.aspx). With both of these services, the author uploads a formatted file, and the company makes a print version available for sale online at Amazon, Barnes & Noble and many other online bookstores. These two companies provide a wide variety of services and have different pricing structures, requiring a separate analysis in the next chapter. It's important to note that they are different; authors must decide for themselves which service best meets their needs and which one (or both) to use to produce their print books.

Don't stop at just an ebook and a print copy—there's so much more! The next thing you're going to want to do is produce an audio version of your book. "But won't that be expensive?" No, it won't cost anything, other than a little of your time. All you need to do is go to Audiobook Creation Exchange (ACX, https://www.acx.com/), which is a website that connects authors with audio producers in the U.S. and U.K. With many people commuting for hours every day and the proliferation of audio players, audio books are probably more popular than you realize. In fact, I sell more audio books than I do print copies! Even better, there is a "royalty share" option on the site. If you select this, you don't have to pay a single thing to have your book converted; an audio producer will do all of the production work for you and will then share in the royalties produced by the sale of the audio book. That's right, the money I make from the sale of my audio books is pure profit. I don't pay a thing; I just listen to the chapters as the producer completes them to ensure they are correctly narrated. If you are sure your book is going to be a hit, you can also find a producer who will convert your book on a fee-based basis instead of the royalty share option. This will let you keep all of the royalties yourself. The handy thing about ACX is it is a subsidiary of Amazon; once the audio book is complete, it will show up on Amazon on its own (with no effort on your part) and will usually merge into the sales page for your book automatically. Your audio book will also be sold through Audible (http://www.audible.com/) and iTunes. For most authors, this is a great way to cheaply and easily get your books into audio. For those who want a more hands-on approach, you can also record and sell your own work directly using sites like Selz, e-Junkie or other services.

You've now got an ebook, a print copy and an audio book. What's next? How about international sales? You're already selling to multiple countries through Amazon (12 at the time of this writing, although they continue to expand their marketplace). Want more? Other online book retailers like Kobo Writing Life can help you reach many more, as they distribute to 170 countries. Sales will be small in most of those countries because their online book sales markets are just starting, but they should continue to grow. Want more? The next step would be to have your book translated into other languages for international readers. The German reading market is large and Spanish is the second most spoken language in the world (ahead of English, which is third). Sites like Babelcube (http://www.babelcube.com) and Proz (http://www.proz.com) are available for translation services. Babelcube is to translation services like ACX is to audio books and has a somewhat similar user interface; Proz is for the project manager who wants to contract directly with an interpreter. For those who want to be a little more hands-off, you can work with an agent or use sites like IPR License or PubMatch to sell the foreign rights for your book.

Another free resource closer to home, especially if your books appeal to a more youthful demographic, is Wattpad (https://www.wattpad.com/). This site is a publishing platform with about 17 million international visitors each month where authors upload books a chapter at a time. A book gains visibility through votes and comments on each chapter. For most authors, Wattpad is about exposing their books to a younger audience than they usually reach with Amazon. If you use Wattpad, make sure you put a buy link for your other books at the bottom of each uploaded chapter.

Got a nonfiction book, especially a self-help book? How about webinars or teleseminars to get the word out? After that comes speaking and coaching/consulting, as well as workshops, seminars, retreats, bootcamps...you get the idea. There are lots of ways to spread your message.

A final opportunity for maximizing your income streams is to collaborate on creative projects. Generally this occurs with other authors in the form of multi-author boxed sets, anthologies or other literary projects, but it could also take place with practitioners of other art forms, like artists and musicians. For example, an author with an action-packed story might combine with a graphic artist to convert the story to a graphic novel.

These ideas aren't meant to describe every possibility, but to spur you to find new income streams that work for you! Want one more? Movies!

Chapter 34 – Preparing your Print Book for Publishing

Aside from the typographic part of the design, it's critically important for authors to properly build their books. There are conventions in book design that are hundreds of years old that must be respected. Simply stated, if your book doesn't look like what's expected, readers aren't going to like it. In addition to using the right fonts, there are many other details that need to be just right, like the treatment of running heads, page numbers, display pages, and so on. If you are unfamiliar with them, it's unlikely you'll get them right.

There are several ways you can design the interior of your print book. The first method is to hire a pro, which is the easiest and most expensive. How do you find a good interior designer? How do you properly evaluate one? You may be surprised to find it's easier to find a good cover designer than it is to find a good interior designer. If you think about it, this makes sense; the cover designer only has to know how to create an effective cover, the interior designer needs to know all the rules of bookmaking. This is even truer for heavily-formatted nonfiction books.

One of the best ways to find designers is by referrals from other authors. If you know someone who has published a book, ask who designed it. Local publishing groups can also be great places to find designers and talk to authors who have worked with them. Trade publications like the *IBPA Independent* from the Independent Book Publishers Association (IBPA) are good sources, as book designers often advertise their services in them. Author services websites will also help authors develop a "publishing team." If you've got a heavily-formatted book, make sure the designers you're querying have produced books like yours before. Ask to see samples or a portfolio of similar books.

The next question is, "How much you should expect to pay for a typical paperback novel?" For most novels, you can expect to pay between $200 and $1,500 for interior design. You are likely to get a very simplified design at the lower end and custom designs for your book at the higher end. Make sure the designer takes responsibility for creating the reproduction files for your printer, and that there's an allowance for "author's alterations," because there are always changes that have to be made. Just like for cover design, make sure you have a signed agreement stating that you will own the copyright to all the work produced, and that you'll be able to get the original application files the designer created once the project is complete.

At the other end of the design spectrum is doing all of the formatting yourself. Beware if you attempt this, as there is a correct order the parts are supposed to be in, and the front matter and back matter need to be entered correctly. If you know and understand how to do them, have at it! If you don't, there are books that will show you how to format a print book, but it's beyond the scope of this book to go into all the facets, and why they are required.

In between these two extremes in terms of both effort and price lies a middle road I much prefer; self-formatting using a template. There are many sites that sell pre-formatted book files. With these, all you do is copy and paste your manuscript into the template, and the template will take care of all the little things for you, including starting chapters on the right page. This is the way I format all my books, using templates purchased from the Book Designer website. The site's operator, Joel Friedlander, has a good selection of easy-to-use templates available to fill the needs of both fiction and nonfiction authors. They are available at http://www.bookdesigntemplates.com/, where you will also get a free construction blueprint guide.

Chapter 35 – Print Books: CreateSpace vs. Ingram Spark

S o, you've got your ebook posted on Amazon and the other ebook retailers, and you have developed the print version of your book. You should already have a cover ready (see Unit 5 if you skipped it earlier). You're ready to decide which print-on-demand company to use.

The choice of whether to use CreateSpace or Ingram Spark is a big consideration, because they offer very different services and fee structures, which will translate into very different royalty payouts. While price is important, the discussion on which is better is a little more complicated than that, and it involves looking at a number of issues. This chapter will address the biggest concerns for most independent authors, based on a 300-page black and white 6"x9"paperback book with cream paper and a gloss finish. The prices listed are what are currently listed on the two companies' websites.

The first two differences are the cost of production and the cost to implement changes. These are very straightforward. At $4.45, CreateSpace costs $0.35 less than Ingram Spark ($4.80) to produce a book. If all other things were equal (they aren't), then CreateSpace would be the obvious choice as you would make more for every copy sold. CreateSpace also doesn't charge if you need to make changes, while Spark charges you $25. If you think you will be updating or revising your book frequently, those charges could add up fast. For a $3.99 ebook on Amazon (70% royalty rate), you'll have to sell about 9 books every time you update your book, just to cover the fee.

The next issue is the cost of setup and the yearly fee. CreateSpace has no setup fee and no yearly fee, while Spark has a $49 setup fee and a $12 yearly fee. If you are a member of the Alliance of Independent Authors, the setup fee is reduced to $37.50, and the yearly fee is waived; however, CreateSpace is still the better deal here.

CreateSpace also comes out on top for ease of use. Uploading your file on CreateSpace is simple, and the process can be completed in less than an hour. In my experience, Spark wasn't as easy. Spark was designed for professionals and reflects that. Although it isn't "difficult" once you figure out how to do it, the learning curve is steeper for the first-time user. Once again, CreateSpace is the winner.

ISBNs are another area where CreateSpace wins, as Spark doesn't offer them; the difference, however, isn't as large as you might think. There are several ways ISBNs can be implemented with CreateSpace. You can get one for free from CreateSpace, but it will list CreateSpace as the imprint and the distributor, so that method isn't recommended. You can also get one for $10, but that still lists CreateSpace as the distributor (although you get to pick your own imprint). A third way is to pay $99 and name both your imprint and distributor, but that is not a great deal. As noted in Chapter 28, authors can purchase ISBNs in bulk and supply them much more cost effectively. Since it's best to supply your own ISBN, this factor is fairly moot.

There are a few issues where Spark is the obvious winner. If you need a hard cover, you have to go with Spark, as CreateSpace doesn't offer this option. Spark will also let a bookseller return copies (if you choose the 55% discount, which will be described later); CreateSpace will not. Finally, if your book has color illustrations, Spark is much cheaper ($8.40 versus $21.85).

Shipping is an issue where there is no clear cut winner. For shipping in the U.S., CreateSpace is the winner for speed of delivery and affordability. Outside of the U.S., though, Spark gets your book to the customer quicker and cheaper, as they have overseas production facilities.

Finally, we come to the issue of discounts, which is a big factor in the decision. Discounts are often confusing and misunderstood by most independent authors, so they need an explanation. Don't worry, I'll be gentle. What's a discount? The discount is the amount that you are discounting the book off the retail price to sell it at a retailer. The retailer and the distributer both get paid from this portion; you get what's left. There is a difference between online sales and sales made through bookstores, so we will look at both of these individually.

First, let's look at sales made through an online distributor like Amazon, Barnes & Noble and Books–A–Million, where most of your print books will probably be sold. For these, CreateSpace takes 40% when you sell on Amazon and 60% for anywhere else. So, for a $15 book, this will result in CreateSpace taking $6 if you sell your book on Amazon and $9 anywhere else. When you subtract the $4.45 cost of production (from the resulting $9 and $6 remainders), you are left with a profit of $4.55 on Amazon sales and $1.55 anywhere else.

Spark offers a 40% discount for online sales. At this discount, you will receive a profit of $4.20 per book sold, regardless of where it is sold (Spark doesn't differentiate between Amazon and other stores). So, for books sold through online retailers, you are better off using CreateSpace for Amazon sales and Spark for everywhere else. You'll earn $4.55 on Amazon with CreateSpace and $4.20 using Spark for books sold at Barnes & Noble, Books-A-Million or any other retailer that orders your book (versus the $1.55 you would have received from CreateSpace). That's a big difference...if you are selling enough books to cover Spark's higher fees.

For books you are trying to stock at brick and mortar stores, Spark offers a 55% discount, although this option won't necessarily result in the stores stocking your book. Barring other merchandising, they will *order* your book if a customer requests it, but they probably won't stock it. From the 55% discount, the bookstores receive a 40% of the retail price (Spark keeps the other 15% for distribution). So if your book retails at $15, the bookstores would buy it from Spark at $9. Spark keeps 15% ($2.25). You would be credited $6.75 ($15–55%) for each sale, from which you would have to deduct the cost of printing the book (4.80), which leaves you a profit of $1.95. This is a little better than the $1.55 you would have received from the CreateSpace expanded distribution option. Of note, with this distribution method, the bookstore makes $6 from the sale of each of your books. If you can merchandise your book well, they *might* consider stocking it.

Most bookstores will tell you they won't stock CreateSpace books. For some of them (especially independent bookstores), not selling CreateSpace books is a matter of principle (they don't want to stock books made by Amazon or its subsidiaries), but for most of them, it's simply a matter of economics. Even though CreateSpace charges the author 60% for distribution beyond Amazon, the bookstores only receive about 25%, because CreateSpace uses Spark for distribution. Spark gets approximately 15% of the cut, and CreateSpace takes about 20%. That leaves 25%, or about $3.75, for the bookstores. That's not enough for a bookstore to stock your book. Table 3 recaps the various features.

In summary, both companies have areas in which they excel. CreateSpace is easy to use and offers fast and inexpensive production and distribution to Amazon customers, especially when shipping within the United States, and doesn't have any setup, change or yearly fees. Spark offers better production and distribution to all retailers that aren't named "Amazon," especially international customers, is cheaper in color and is the only company you can use for hard cover books.

Authors need to evaluate their own situations and determine which company best meets their needs. It might be CreateSpace, it might be Spark and it might be a combination of both. For the beginning author, CreateSpace may be a better supplier to start out with until you get your feet under you, as it is easier to use and doesn't charge any fees. This may be important for beginning authors who might have to update their stories frequently.

Features	CreateSpace	Ingram Spark
Cost per copy B&W	$4.45	$4.80
Cost per copy color	$21.85	$8.40
Changes	$0	$25
Cost of setup	$0	$49
Yearly fee	$0	$12
Ease of setup	Very easy	Learning
ISBN	Yes	No
Hard cover	No	Yes
Returns	No	Yes
Discount	40/60%	40/55%
Shipping	Best to U.S.	Best for Intl.

Table 3. Feature Breakdown on January 10, 2015

Increasing Your Reach

Your book is published, so it's time to accelerate the marketing push. Don't be shy; if you don't promote your book, it's highly unlikely anyone else will either. You've already been working on your platform, and you should continue to promote your book on all of your social media sites. In addition to your ongoing efforts, this unit will look at other ways you can increase your reach.

Chapter 36 – 5 Marketing Notes to Help You Refocus

You must continually evaluate how well each of your sites is furthering your message. Are they effectively promoting your book? If not, give a different avenue a chance. This chapter will address five pieces of recent research by Patel that will help you refocus your marketing efforts if they aren't performing as well as you hoped.

First, hopefully you have been working on that email list because email marketing has been shown to be much better at converting buyers than social media. How much better? Its return on investment is 4,300%, or about an order of magnitude greater than social media alone. What does this mean to you? It means email marketing is much more effective than social media marketing, and you should spend more of your time and money on it. If you haven't already, you need to get that website email capture form up and running ASAP!

Second, YouTube has the highest engagement and lowest bounce rate (how fast visitors leave) of any of the social media sites. As such, YouTube deserves more of your social media time and effort than you (or I) might have otherwise thought. This information also means that it's worth the effort to create and add videos to your sites. The more video content you design, the more you'll engage your potential customers. The research is clear; if you want the most-engaged traffic, make some videos!

Third, Facebook drives more referrals than any other social media site. What does that mean? It means your Facebook site will probably be sending more traffic to your website (or Amazon) than any of your other sites. Even though page interaction is shrinking, Facebook still drives more traffic than any other social media site. Its closest rival, Pinterest, is far behind.

Speaking of Pinterest, the fourth research finding is that each Pinterest pin is worth 78 cents. Pinterest is a site that doesn't work well for everyone, but for some lucky genres, it works very well. In general, Pinterest has a high bounce rate and low engagement, which indicates most people just pass through without becoming engaged in any of the pictures or boards. If you are writing about topics that translate well into pictures, like food, crafts, photography, weddings and travel, though, Pinterest may work well for you. It also works well for genres that are targeted at women, as Pinterest's membership is over 80% female.

Although the site may hold promise for some authors, it must be noted that posting happens much more slowly on Pinterest than on other social media sites. Unlike Twitter, where posts quickly fade away, Pinterest visits actually increase as time goes on, and most posts don't start generating revenue until more than two months after the initial pinning. If you use Pinterest, you have to be patient.

The fifth research point is a direct contrast to the fourth. If you are going to use Twitter, things on that site happen NOW! In fact, 65% of Twitter users expect a response in under two hours, and if you don't respond quickly, you're just as quickly forgotten. There's a lot to gain by a quick response, and a lot to lose if you don't. If you're going to use Twitter, stay on top of it!

Chapter 37 –Networking and Why You Must

One important topic for independent authors that doesn't get much press is networking. Although authors sometimes tend to be hermits, you need to learn to reach out to others authors and members of the industry, as the benefits of networking far outweigh the drawbacks. What benefits? Some of the biggest are joint marketing opportunities, keeping up with industry best practices and getting answers to questions from experienced authors.

Where do you find networking opportunities? There are plenty of venues to meet new people, like social media groups (Facebook, Goodreads and LinkedIn), professional groups (Romance Writers of America and the Alliance for Independent Authors), and professional workshops/conventions and support forums. Authors just need to remember as they explore these interactions that there are rules that must be followed with all of them, and it's important to respect others and play by the rules. Let's take a look at some of the opportunities for networking.

One great opportunity is to join a writing group. Regardless of where you are, there are probably several organizations in the area that exist to help writers develop their craft. Whether you are looking for a genre-specific group or one with a broader reach, writing associations are extremely worthwhile. Look for organizations that offer a sense of community.

Joining a critique group is another way to strengthen your writing skills and get new eyes on your work in progress. Having trusted readers who will tell you what's working (and what isn't) can help you develop a manuscript that's polished and ready for outside eyes. One thing to note is not all critique groups are a good fit for everyone, and not everyone is a good fit for every critique group. If you aren't getting what you need from a critique group, find a new group. Also, if you don't like the idea of sharing early drafts, a critique group may not be the right thing for you; writing buddies and a few trusted beta readers might be a better option.

Depending on your genre, there are a number of conferences and conventions you can attend. Conventions are great for networking with other authors, promoting (and selling) your books to fans and developing yourself through panels and discussions held there. I've made great friends at conventions and have had tremendous promotional opportunities by speaking on a wide variety of topics at them. I can't recommend attending them enough!

Another way to meet new people is to enter contests, as they are a great way to get feedback from readers other than your writing/critique group partners and friends and family. In addition to the extra feedback, you may win a prize, which is a great way to show agents your work is valuable and being recognized.

Do I need to mention social media as a way of networking? By this point, I hope not. The key to social media is that it *is* social; by its very nature it helps grow your circle of friends and your network. As already discussed, social media is a great place to connect with other writers, agents, editors and readers, as well as an outstanding venue to keep up with the latest news and trends.

Chapter 38 – Book Reviews and Other Things That Suck

An unreviewed book on Amazon or Goodreads is one of the saddest things you'll see; however, the mere mention of the word "reviews" is guaranteed to make authors cringe. While most would love to have large numbers of 5-star reviews, how to get them is often a mystery. Some authors may even cross ethical lines and pay review mills for them, trade reviews with other authors or establish fake accounts to review their own books and/or trash someone else's. Not only are they unethical, they can also get you kicked off Amazon, your largest source of revenue. Before we discuss how to get reviews, I want to make one point clear: I don't think you should pay for reviews. Ever.

There are many sites that will post reviews for pay. Although there are a few reputable sites, many are rip-offs, or run by people with questionable morals. Why would someone pay for reviews? Because the biggest problem independent publishers face is getting attention for their book, and reviews can help sell books. If paying for reviews can help sell books, why am I so set against it? Because I don't think paid reviews are honest to the readers. And, when it comes out you've purchased reviews (and things always get out these days), your readers will assume all of your book reviews have been purchased. Rather than take a chance on your books, they may look other places to make their purchase.

If you're not going to pay for reviews, how will you get them? You're going to have to work for them. The process of getting reviews and testimonials is a challenging one; however, it is also one of the best exercises authors can get in book marketing. Not only will gathering reviews teach you how books are sold, but it will also show how your book is being received. There are a number of high-stress, high-energy ways people promote as the "best" way to get reviews (I've tried many of them); I'd like to suggest the following seven ways of getting reviews while still maintaining your sanity:

1. First, before your book comes out, offer advanced reader copies to selected fans and reviewers you've established friendships with. Always send a personal email, not a mass mailing, as asking for a review is like querying an agent. Anything that smells of mass-mailing gets an automatic "no."

2. Promote your books in other ways, like guest blogposts, spotlights and interviews.

3. Continue your normal interactions on your chosen social media sites. Push content at least 80% of the time and make some friends. That way, when you ask for reviews, you will have people that who and respect you. Some will even read and recommend your books.

4. Continue to grow your readership with your blog, website or newsletter. Grow your email list of people who like, respect and follow you by putting out great content and freebies. Once again, some will read and recommend your books when you (infrequently) ask them to.

5. Recommend books you love and talk about how you reviewed them because all authors need reviews for their books. If you see a book you love only has a handful of reviews, write one. Remember, that could be you. A small portion of your readers will "get it" and do the same for you.

6. After you get 25 or so reviews, don't worry about them anymore. While there are some newsletters that require a certain amount of reviews to be eligible (Fussy Librarian, Kindle Nation Daily, and Ereader News Today), having more reviews than that isn't necessary to have good sales.

7. Put all the energy you would have wasted begging for reviews into writing your next book. That will do more to help drive sales.

Why not give away lots of free copies to reviewers on sites like Goodreads to get reviews? Because most giveaways generate very few reviews. Not only that, scammers use these sites to get free hard copies they can sell on EBay. There is also a bizarre reviewer subculture that revels in giving nasty reviews to books they haven't read. They'll do nothing more than look at a few lines of the "look inside" sample or simply reword other negative reviews. Still others will buy and then return an ebook within minutes so they don't have to pay for it and can get the "Verified Purchase" stamp from Amazon on their one-word, one-star review.

Why do they do this? I don't know for sure, but some people appear to be trying to rack up an enormous number of reviews, which makes them eligible to get free products to review. Others are probably just mean people who are leading terrible lives.

Speaking of bad reviews, what should you do when you get one? The answer is "nothing." The first time you get a bad review, it's going to feel like a personal attack. Even though you're going to feel like yelling at the reviewer or explaining why he or she is wrong, you're not going to do anything. It's just unprofessional. You can't win the fight; all you'll end up doing is bringing yourself down to their level. Remember I said that some people write bad reviews on purpose? They won't care what you think. If anything, they'll be happy they got a rise out of you. Take a look at the review of my book *Janissaries* on October 1, 2014 in Figure 1.

Figure 1. Amazon Reviews for "Janissaries"

I'm not sure what else the anonymous "Amazon Customer," who hadn't even purchased the book, could have said in five words to make my book sound worse. You know what I did? Nothing, and the next day the other review showed up, which was along the lines of most of the other reviews my

book *Janissaries* received and was from someone that had actually purchased the book, giving the review additional credibility. The only thing getting a bad review means is you're a published author. Every author gets bad reviews.

But don't bad reviews bring down sales? No, not always. In fact, sometimes bad reviews can actually stimulate buying. If you react to them, though, you risk escalating the attacks, potentially doing real damage to your sales. These days, reviews aren't as important as they used to be. Book discovery happens in hundreds of ways, both online and offline. Word of mouth is still the most important means of advertising, so it's better to work on buzz than reviews.

Please note I'm not telling readers (or authors) not to write reviews! Book reviews still have a place, especially reviews from book bloggers, but you don't need to obsess about them. You can live with fewer than you think.

Chapter 39 – 8 Other Ways to Promote Your Book

Hundreds of thousands of new books are added to Amazon and Smashwords every year, and independent authors have to compete against authors with big budgets and publicity teams to spread the word. Like many other aspects of self-publishing, there are plenty of ways you can reach readers on a budget if you are creative and work smarter, not harder. This chapter will show you eight ways:

1. **Interviews.** In addition to reviews and blogs, interviews are a great way to increase your book's reach, especially when broadcast in audio formats like radio and podcasts. Internet radio is an expanding media, and there are thousands of radio stations and podcasts out there. Each of these has programming that requires a continuous parade of guests and experts. March in that parade! Don't just think about review-like interviews, look beyond that to how subjects in your book could be adapted into an interesting discussion or interview. Then, find out which shows would benefit from having you as a guest and pitch yourself to the shows' producers. If nothing else, you have the experience of being an independent author; you could always pitch a show on the trials and tribulations of "going it alone."

How do you find radio shows that might be a good fit for your subject matter? Take a look at the Radio Locator database (http://radio-locator.com/). Billed as the most comprehensive radio station search engine on the internet, it has links to over 14,100 web pages and over 9,700 audio streams from radio stations in the U.S. and around the world. You can search the Radio Locator database for radio stations by geography or format and then connect to the station's website, where you can find out about show topics and get the producer's contact information.

Interested in podcasts? Take a look at the "Podcasts" section of the iTunes store where you can search for different keywords related to your book. There are a wide variety of shows...probably more than you'll be able to track on a recurring basis. If you find yourself overwhelmed, you can subscribe to the Radio Guest List (http://www.radioguestlist.com/), a free booking service that sends you a daily email with current radio, podcast, and television publicity opportunities.

2. **Sponsorships.** These days, many of the internet radio shows and podcasts are produced at the host's expense. Because of this, many are now selling sponsorships to help offset production costs. These spots are normally short messages either read by the host or pre-recorded by the sponsor, which are then played during the show. Usually the cost is nominal; however, they can have a great impact if you target shows that reach your book's audience.

3. **Free Samples.** In addition to the free samples you offered on Amazon and the other ebook retailers, you can offer free samples in other places, like your website, to increase its draw and reach. Got an audio book? SoundCloud allows you to create a free sample that you can embed in your website, in blog posts and anywhere else you have a social presence. You can also link it directly to your audio book's buying page to make it easy for customers to purchase. This method is better than the "free audio sample" feature on Audible because your customers don't have to visit Audible to hear it.

4. **The One Minute Trailer.** It is becoming more frequent for books to launch with a trailer. This is a great way to generate interest, as long as it isn't too long. Most people have a minute that they can give you, but you probably won't be able to keep their interest much longer than that. Keep the trailer to one minute and link to it on your social media sites. You can even put the link to your trailer (along with the link to your free audio sample) in your email signature to maximize its reach.

5. **Promotional Cards**. Sometimes you are constrained by space or size in how much product you can have at an event, and books are bulky and heavy to carry, especially if you have a number of titles. Bringing a large selection to an event may be very inconvenient. Digital audio books can be difficult to sell at an event because they're not a tangible product. When you aren't able to display a product, a small card can be used to promote your product. Do you attend conferences and/or conventions? Have promotional cards in your display for people to take with them. With the proliferation of ebook readers, these can serve as handy reminders of your book for when customers get home and make their purchases. You can easily get promotional cards made through online printing services like VistaPrint (http://www.vistaprint.com).

6. **Affiliations**. Are you part of a group, club, network or association? How about an alumni club? Does it have a newsletter? Many have sections dedicated to member news which you can exploit. These types of opportunities are a great source of free advertising, yet they're often overlooked.

7. **Conventions**. As mentioned in Chapter 37, attending conventions is a great way to promote your books, especially if you give talks or participate in panels. The opportunities to interact with fans are incredible, and they have helped me develop a number of long-lasting friends. There is a reason I will be speaking at ten conventions this year—it works! Even if you only go as an attendee (and not a guest speaker), conventions are still wonderful promotional opportunities.

8. **Contests and Awards**. Have you ever thought about entering a book contest or applying for a writing

award? Not only would winning a contest or award serve as a great publicity hook, but it also might lead to a publishing contract, and it would build your confidence as a writer. Being able to say your book won first place in a competition would be a great lead-in for your next query letter or book blurb; however, it is less important to win the contest than it is to get your name out there. As such, even the smaller contests are worth entering. Beware, however, of contests that have big fees attached, or ones that serve as money-makers for agencies.

Even audio books have awards. For example, the Audio Publishers Association (APA) holds its annual Audie Awards where it recognizes distinction in audio books and spoken word entertainment across 30 different categories. Although the entry fee for this competition is stiff ($100 for APA members; $175 for non-members), this sort of recognition would go a *long* way in letting the world know about your audio book.

What You Must Do Next

Is your book selling like gang-busters? Great! Skip this intro and get back to work! For the rest of you...you say your book isn't selling as well as you hoped? Should you panic? Yes! Yell and scream for two minutes. Go ahead, I'll wait.

Now, if you're done screaming, it's important to note that if your first book doesn't sell as well as you hope (and most first books don't), that doesn't mean you're a failure; it just means you're normal. This is the point where most authors will pack it in and say, "I guess writing wasn't for me after all. I just don't have what it takes." If that is what you think, you're probably right, and you *will* fail. Only a small part of an author's success is due to his or her actual writing talent; marketing and other factors (like an author's determination) usually play much greater roles. Many of the "popular" books today are ones that have good hooks or great marketing campaigns; they are successful *in spite* of the writing, not because of it. Similarly, there are countless great books out there we'll never hear of because the authors couldn't market them well. Still want to be a successful author? This unit will help get you there.

Chapter 40 – The Power of Writing More

One of the most important things you, as an author, can do to increase your sales is to write more books. Why is that? Four reasons. First, you are seen as more of a professional if you have more books. You look like you are in the business of writing, so your work is probably going to be edited and worth reading. As such, readers will see it as a "safe" option to spend their money on.

Second, readers like to fall in love with authors and read all of their books. If an author only has a single book for sale, readers won't want to invest in the author because they don't pass the "what next?" test. The reader will subconsciously worry about the fact that, if I like this author, he/she doesn't have anything else for me to read when I finish this book. Maybe it's just not worth getting hooked on the author to start with. Remember, marketing is all about relationships.

Third, having more books increases your chances of being found. Despite your best intentions (and marketing efforts), Amazon and all of the other ebook retailers are crowded stores, and it's possible some readers missed your first offering. By putting a second book on the site, you double your chances of being found. When you are found, readers will usually go back and start at the beginning of the series. For example, the month my fourth book came out, the first three books all had their second best sales months ever as readers went back to start at the beginning of the series. The fourth reason is related to the third; once readers gets hooked on a series, they are probably going to stay with you to the end. With a series, readers become attached to a central character or characters, and the subsequent books sell themselves. The momentum carries over from book to book, as readers want to know what happens next. In most cases, you don't even have to market the sequel to "sell" it to your fans; they will buy the book because they are already invested. All you need to do is send them an email to let them know when it is going to be out (you captured their email addresses way back in Chapter 10, right?)

Chapter 41 – You Must Improve!

A s a professional author, it is important for you to continue to learn and grow in your craft. It will help keep the readers you already have, while continuing to attract new ones. What is the best way to learn? Whatever works best for you. There are a number of ways to approach your professional development.

The first and most obvious method is to take classes. There is more to writing (especially fiction writing) than you may realize. Many people won't care about things like character arcs as long as the story is good, but other people will, and they will hold you accountable for your lack of technical merit. If you don't know what a character or story arc is, you might need to invest some time and energy studying the craft. There are classes available on everything from dialogue to plot development. Not only will you learn about a topic in class, you will meet other writers and have opportunities to interact with other people in the industry. Remember the discussion on networking in Chapter 37? This is a great way to meet other authors who care about writing well.

Another opportunity is to attend writers' retreats. At these events, you usually get a chance to meet established writers who will share their experiences and sometimes pass on their list of industry contacts, giving you an advantage over other authors that don't have them. Retreats are good for both novice and seasoned writers, as they give authors opportunities to complete their current manuscripts or jumpstart new projects. Just like going to a conference, you will have contact with industry professionals that could result in the break you're looking for.

You can develop yourself and network with other writers from the comfort of your own home by following other people's blogs and sharing comments on them. There are plenty of bloggers who write about the industry and give tips on how to become a better writer. You can improve your craft by following these sites and reading their posts; if you enter the discussion, you also have the opportunity to interact with other professionals who will remember your name. Obviously, you should conduct yourself professionally; being courteous and adding good content will get you accepted into the network of professionals and will attract attention to your blog and the projects that you're promoting.

Your goal is to strengthen your writing skills; the fact that most of these tools will help you strengthen your platform as well is sheer serendipity. You want to grow and develop yourself as a writer. You can do it in person through classes and events or over the web by blogging, guest posting, commenting and tweeting. When you are the one posting, make sure you research your topic thoroughly and provide good content; this will also help you grow. Follow agents and editors and check out their tweets to stay abreast of industry changes. By doing all of this, you will not only become a better writer, you will also become more knowledgeable about the writing industry.

Chapter 42 – 5 Reasons Why Your Book Isn't Selling

If you've done everything in this book, there is a good chance your book will be selling, as these are the same strategies I used to sell almost 40,000 books in my first year as an author. Not all independent publishers do that well; in fact, most do not. While many authors attribute sales to luck or timing, it's not about either of these things. Having stellar sales revolves around following a set of best practices, both before your book is published and after it's on the market. If you're not selling, this chapter points out five of the most likely reasons. Although they won't kill your career (remember, only you can do that), these items will keep you from getting the level of sales you want:

1. **There is no market for your book.** Just because you wrote a book doesn't mean you will automatically have readers. Before you write, do some research! How is your genre selling? Who is your competition? What are they doing? As a business person, you have to know your market if you want to have good sales.

2. **You don't have a good book cover.** Customers only spend seconds looking at book covers, most of which are now online thumbnail-size images. A professionally-designed cover is a must!

3. **Your book is poorly edited.** Traditionally published books take months and even *years* of planning, editing and formatting. This process results in a high quality end-product. Don't take editing shortcuts to get your books to market quickly or cheaply; make sure they are properly edited. There are at least 300,000 books published each year. With all of that competition, you want your book to be the best you can make it.

4. **Your book is priced inappropriately.** In order for your book to sell well, it has to be priced in accordance with similar titles. If your book is priced at $19.99 when competing titles are only $9.99, you're probably not going to be selling many books. This is especially true if you are a new author.

5. **You quit (or never started) marketing.** Marketing a book is an ongoing, long-term commitment. If you want to sell, you have to continue to generate awareness and interest in your product. It may not happen as quickly as you want, but don't let your-

self get frustrated or discouraged. Success may not happen overnight, but it will happen if you continue to write good books. Don't get mad, get writing!

Chapter 43 – Final Words

Writing is the best job ever. The best. There's no commute to contend with, no annoying boss to answer to and you don't even have to shave if you don't want to. Writing can even get you out of those pesky obligations your significant other mistakenly signed you up for ("Sorry, I'm on a deadline.") What's the downside?

The same as any other job, you've got to show up. If you don't write, you don't publish. Unlike a "normal" job, it's easy to get distracted if you work at home, so you have to be self-motivated to be successful. There's only you...you have to be your own boss and make it work. How do you do that? Here are some ideas:

1. Make a schedule and stick to it. Quantify the schedule with either an amount of time to be spent or number of words to be written. Refrain from doing other chores when you are supposed to be writing.

2. Make sure the people around you know your writing schedule and word count goals so they can support you (i.e., not bother you during those times) and hold you accountable.

3. Make sure your "work" time includes time to maintain your social media platform. A reasonable balance is one hour of social media (Angry Birds doesn't count) for every three hours of writing.

4. Continue to develop yourself and your craft. Include time in your schedule to read books and blogs about writing, take a class or work on an area you want to improve. Just like you have training in other jobs, you have to continue to grow as a professional writer.

5. Most importantly, always be focused on writing the next book. That is what is going to continue to pay the bills.

6. Still have questions? Check out all of the services available at http://chriskennedypublishing.com. While you're there, sign up for my email list!

Remember, hoping you will be lucky and that your book will be the "next big thing" are not viable business strategies. It is absolutely possible to have a career in writing, but as with any other career, that takes work. You need to have a long-term business plan that includes professional development, marketing and writing in order to be successful. Okay...you've done enough reading and professional development for today—get back to work on that next book!

* * * * *

Works Cited

A Charman-Anderson, Suw. "Penguin And Author Solutions Sued For Deceptive Practices." *Forbes*. Forbes.com. 7 May 2013. Web. 10 Jan. 2015.

Chrzan, Quinn. "Pinterest: A Review of Social Media's Newest Sweetheart." *Engauge.com*. Engauge.com. 2 Jan. 2013. Web. 10 Jan. 2015.

Cooper, Belle Beth. "7 Powerful Facebook Statistics You Should Know for a More Engaging Facebook Page." *Buffer Social*. Buffer. 23 Jul 2013. Web. 10 Jan. 2015.

Davidson, Neil. "If you have a video your Kickstarter project is 85% more likely to succeed." *MWP Results Driven Video*. My Web Presenters Limited. 30 Jul. 2013. Web. 10 Jan. 2015.

"Editorial Rates." *Editorial Freelancers Association*. Editorial Freelancers Association. Jun 2012. Web. 10 Jan. 2015.

Epstein, Joseph. "Think You Have a Book in You? Think Again." *New York Times*. The New York Times Company. 28 Sep. 2002. Web. 10 Jan. 2015.

Gardner, Rachelle. "Pinterest: 13 Things Writers Should Know." *Rachelle Gardner*. 5 Mar. 2012. Web. 10 Jan. 2015.

King, Stephen. *On Writing.* London: Hodder & Stoughton, 2001. Print.

Mullenweg, Matt. "WordPress 3.3 "Sonny."" *Wordpress.org.* Wordpress.org. 12 Dec. 2011. Web. 10 Jan. 2015.

Patel, Neil. "Five Shocking Facts That Will Change Your Entire Approach to Social Media." *KISSmetrics.com.* KISSmetrics.com. n.d. Web. 10 Jan. 2015.

Warnock, Brittany. "Start Your Blog or Site in 5 Minutes with Wordpress." *Bluehost Blog.* Bluehost Inc. n.d. Web. 10 Jan. 2015.

Connect with Chris Kennedy

Website: http://chriskennedypublishing.com/

Facebook:
https://www.facebook.com/chriskennedypublishing.biz

Twitter: @ChrisKennedy110

Want to be immortalized in a future book?

Join the Red Shirt List on the blog!

Did you like this book?

Please write a review!

About the Author

A bestselling Science Fiction/Fantasy author and speaker, Chris Kennedy is a former naval aviator with over 3,000 hours flying attack and reconnaissance aircraft. Chris is currently working as an Instructional Systems Designer for the Navy and is an advisory board member of Hampton Roads Writers.

Chris' full length novels include the "Occupied Seattle" military fiction duology, the "Theogony" science fiction trilogy and the "War for Dominance" fantasy trilogy. Chris is currently working on "The Search for Gram," the fourth book set in the Theogony universe.

CPSIA information can be obtained at www.ICGtesting.com
Printed in the USA
LVOW04s1923170215

427237LV00031B/1280/P

9 781942 936008